Counseling from Profiles

A Casebook
for the
Differential Aptitude Tests

George K. Bennett

Harold G. Seashore

Alexander G. Wesman

Board of Cooperative Educational Services
10 Cedar Street
Valhalla, N. Y. 10595

The Psychological Corporation
New York, New York

Printed in U.S.A.
Ψ Reg. U.S. Pat. Off.

65-425B

Since the preparation of this casebook, the *Differential Aptitude Tests* have been revised; Forms L and M were published in 1963. The revisions include some changes in format, and in the scoring formula; the battery has also been newly normed. Raw scores on tests of Forms L and M are not equivalent to raw scores on counterpart tests of the earlier Forms A and B, which are reported in this casebook.

However, the content of the new forms has remained basically unchanged from the earlier forms. Accordingly, *in terms of percentile ranks,* the same counseling interpretations which were appropriate to performance on the earlier forms are fully as appropriate to the revised forms. The meaning of high, average, or low percentile rank on the tests is unaltered.

How This Booklet Came To Be Written

SINCE the publication of the *Differential Aptitude Tests*[1] in 1947 we have had frequent inquiries as to how counselors in schools could use the test profiles more effectively. Some of our counseling colleagues found they could use the *Differential Aptitude Test* materials easily and proceeded to do so. Others reported that they were accustomed to thinking in terms of single-score IQs, plus a few other test scores, and that they found it difficult to work with a test profile. One director of guidance reported that his staff members found themselves uncomfortable in the presence of eight scores and wanted to discontinue use of the battery. He was equally concerned because these counselors felt that a single score was much easier to interpret, when in fact this is not true.

The *Differential Aptitude Tests* are included in training courses for counselors in quite a few universities, both to illustrate basic concepts in measurement and as laboratory materials in test administration. Requests for teaching aids to accompany them have come from professors of psychological and educational measurement. Supervisors of large staffs in city and state systems also have suggested that we bring together the experience of counselors in a book.

An obvious way of meeting these needs was to seek the help of competent counselors around the country. Letters accordingly were written to several dozen directors of guidance or counselors. They were given only a very general invitation to submit cases, in brief form, illustrating the various uses of the *Differential Aptitude Tests* in their schools. This book presents 30 cases selected from among more than 50 submitted by counselors in nine schools.

---

[1]George K. Bennett, Harold G. Seashore, Alexander G. Wesman. *The Differential Aptitude Tests*. New York: The Psychological Corporation, 1947.

There are two reasons why this booklet is focused on the *Differential Aptitude Tests*. First, as the authors of the battery, we have a genuine interest in the proper use of the *Differential Aptitude Tests*. Second, we believe that a series of cases built around a particular testing program can be of *general* value. The readers of this booklet will see a wide variety of cases, with interrelated socio-economic and educational problems ranging from simple to complex, illustrating differing degrees of success and failure of counseling. This variety of case material anchored to a common testing program should be helpful in the training of the counselor, whether in a university or on the job.

These cases are much too brief to serve alone as general training material for counselors. After reading a few of the cases in manuscript, one teacher of counseling methods remarked that these were quite acceptable as a "first start" but that what is really needed is a collection of complete case histories, including recorded dialogue, so written that they could serve as an all-around foundation for the training of new counselors and the upgrading of practicing counselors. We have deliberately kept the reports brief because we do not expect this booklet to play a major role in the training of counselors in all aspects of their job. These examples can contribute to professional growth in the special area of test-profile interpretation; but they are not expected to be very helpful in teaching such areas as interviewing, the use of occupational information, or knowledge of psychometric theory. The reader is asked to keep in mind the particular purpose of the booklet and to consider it as only one chapter in a series of chapters, from many sources, which are needed by both counselors-in-training and practicing counselors.

How the Cases Are Reported

All names are fictitious. In order to protect still further the confidential counseling relationship, the name of the school is omitted from each case report.

The *problem* is stated as it was presented at the beginning of counseling. The reader will recognize that the initial statement is not always the real problem or the whole problem.

Test results are given with an indication of the grade in which they were secured. The *Differential Aptitude Test* profile is plotted, while for other tests as much information is given as seems relevant to the reporting. In a few cases the years of testing for IQs in the lower grades and the names of the tests used were not recorded.

The *counselor's report* is usually presented almost verbatim as submitted by the counselor; some cases had to be rewritten by the editors because the contributors presented only essential facts and records in a telegraphic style. There was no attempt to force the cases into the same style or degree of completeness.

The *editors' comments* follow the counselor's report. There is no systematic pattern for these comments. We have tried to set down ideas stimulated by the case and to write about them in a way that would be helpful to counselors, counselor-trainers and students. Sometimes counseling techniques are discussed. At other times problems of measurement are broached. Our aim has been to stimulate discussion leading to clarification of viewpoints and methods; this may require a return to the basic literature on measurement for background. In some instances, educational viewpoints and curricular and social organizations are criticized or reinforced. The reader will readily recognize that some of the paragraphs under a particular case might well have been written in connection with another. There is some repetition which, we hope, is proportionate to the importance of the issues.

And so we send the cases of Charles White, Blanche Ridge, Peter Ellis, and the other boys and girls to you for your thoughtful consideration. We hope they will arouse stimulating associations and questions as you read them.[2]

GEORGE K. BENNETT
HAROLD G. SEASHORE
ALEXANDER G. WESMAN

New York, August 1951

---

[2]The cases appearing in this booklet are very real boys and girls, especially to the counselors who were so kind as to report their experiences with them. We are grateful for their fine cooperation.

Dover, New Jersey. J. Dale Weaver, Guidance Director.

East Hartford, Connecticut. Franklyn A. Graff, Guidance Director.

Gary, Indiana. Dr. Isabelle V. Jones, Department of Educational Research; Russell Anderson, Frances Huddleston, Mildred Polak, and Olive Greensfelder, Counselors.

New Castle, Pennsylvania. Elmer Delancy, Psychologist; Marjorie R. Nelson, Guidance Director.

Oak Ridge, Tennessee. Bertis Capehart, Director of Guidance; Sarah Ketron, Counselor.

Springfield, Massachusetts. Cleal Cowing, Assistant Director, Guidance, Placement, and Adult Education Department.

White Plains, New York. Clarence Noyce, Cleo Richardson, and Douglas Dillenbach, High School Counselors.

Worcester, Massachusetts. Dr. Thomas Christensen, Director of Guidance; M. Kathleen Burns, Kathryn Stafford, and Albert Stead, Counselors.

Yonkers, New York. Dr. Robert E. Carey, Director, Bureau of Guidance; Mabel Heep, Counselor.

Some Notes on Counseling from Profiles

Selected Cases Do Not Validate Tests

THE basic validation of the *Differential Aptitude Tests* necessarily rests on the accumulating studies made with small and large groups in a considerable variety of academic and occupational fields. These are reported in the various supplements to the Manual and in the professional journals. The cases in this booklet are not to be considered validation studies, although it is obvious that if the test battery contributes appreciably to counseling of individual cases, the evidence of such usefulness is a contribution toward more general test validation. It is our belief that the *Differential Aptitude Tests* provided important information about each of the cases reported. This is not to say that the tests presented perfect information or complete information, or information that could always be translated into action.

Fortunately our counselors presented no cases in which they had made arguments for differential guidance based on very small differences between test scores. We wish we could believe that their sophistication is representative of all counselors. We can make better sense out of our cases when we do not attach significance to small differences in test scores and when we do not place full responsibility for all the decisions or lack of decisions on the test battery.

Any counselor with good basic training who has handled as many and as varied cases as these will certainly have developed in the art of using multiple test scores. These cases, then, are examples of how test data can be used. The counseling rests on an assumption of satisfactory validity, but the cases are not validation studies per se.

In Some Cases Tests Are Not Important

The reader probably does not need to be reminded that there are cases in which test data are not needed, where counseling can proceed without them. Consider, for example, the able student doing very satisfactory work who needs counseling because of his shyness and his inability to ask a girl to the junior prom. We doubt that tests of aptitudes or achievement are of much help in this situation.

There are other cases in which it is clear, on the basis of the school record, that abilities and achievement are not the matter at issue. Sometimes rather deep-seated emotional problems, perhaps even needing psychiatric attention, underlie the counseling problem. In such instances it may be helpful if the counselor has a rather complete psychometric history of the person, although in many of these cases elaborate testing would not be necessary. Of course, if a school regularly schedules the *Differential Aptitude Tests* for all members of certain classes, say, the ninth grade, it will have these data available should any crisis occur in the student's life. More often than not, the psychometric data will be of value, but there always will be counseling situations in which tests are of little or no importance.

Ability Tests May Only Be Verifiers

Frequently tests of aptitudes or abilities act only as verifiers of what is already known and are valuable only insofar as they enable the next steps to be taken with greater confidence. For example, the boy with all of his test scores above the 85th percentile probably has the ability to succeed in almost any college and any course he chooses. The counseling problem here is one of eliciting and verifying interests, opportunities, and other relevant factors. Much counseling of this type can go on even if tests are not available. Sometimes in the case of the boy who has no clear-cut career objectives, the main job of the counselor may be to delay the student's making highly specific decisions regarding his career and to urge the student to enter college with the idea of further career exploration during his first year or two.

Why No Composite Scores?

Counselors have asked the authors why they have not provided norms for a composite score on the *Differential Aptitude Tests*. Actually, the *Differential Aptitude Tests* were developed as a purposeful step away from the single all-embracing, comprehensive score.

Some inquiries are based on the desire to relate the performance on the *DAT* to the well-established concept of the IQ or even to compare the results with some particular IQ that is already in the record. Other counselors feel that they would like to combine some of the scores to get a measure of "scholastic aptitude." They recognize that the numerous validity coefficients reported in the Manual have established certain of the tests in the battery as measures of all-around scholastic aptitude, and they propose a special weighted index for this purpose—usually one based on the Verbal Reasoning, Numerical Ability, and Sentences tests.[3]

The authors of the battery believe that neither of these arguments in favor of a comprehensive score is sufficiently convincing. Cases reported in this little book demonstrate repeatedly the importance of not obscuring the significance of reliable score differences by combining them to yield a single composite figure. Actually, little is to be gained from any such composite in comparison with what we inevitably lose. Although we will have much to learn about how to use patterns effectively and how to compare one pattern with another in simple terms, it is fairly clear that counseling from profiles is here to stay.

What the IQ Can Hide

A striking feature of some of the cases in this booklet, and one which has been called to our attention by many counselors, is that the use of a battery of tests illuminates cases which were quite obscure when only a single-score IQ was available. For example, two students who are of the same chronological age and earn the same total score on a test composed of verbal and numerical items, will receive the same IQ. Yet one of these students may have answered all the numerical items correctly and done but indifferently well on the verbal items; the other may have answered few of the numerical items correctly, but handled the verbal items well. Can anyone doubt that these boys, described as identical by the IQ, will perform quite differently in a course in algebra—or that they may need to consider different careers?

There is another way in which such IQs can mislead us. The typical so-called intelligence test is highly loaded with verbal material; some such tests have numerical or quantitative content leading to a separate score. Usually the single score is a weighting of the verbal and other miscellaneous items that are in the test. With all due respect to the usefulness of these tests for certain purposes, and certainly to their histor-

---

[3]The Manual presents the coefficients of correlation between the eight *DAT* scores and several well-known tests of mental ability. In general, the Verbal score correlates highly with verbally-loaded intelligence tests. (Fifth Research Report, Fall 1951.)

ical importance in the development of counseling, we should now face the fact that "intelligence" has many aspects, not all of which have yet been adequately described.

It is becoming more and more apparent that a sensible attempt to obtain a rating on more than one of the facets of the mind will provide more meaningful information for guidance purposes than will a single score. In several cases in this booklet it will be seen that youngsters were considered to be of generally poor caliber because their low IQs and their deficient language skills corroborated each other in the classroom. When the *Differential Aptitude Tests* were given, the Verbal and the Language Usage scores may in turn have supported the IQ and the language achievement scores reported previously—but interesting strengths appeared at the other points of the profile.

A considerable amount of circular reasoning has gone on in many schools because of undifferentiated descriptions. Perhaps a pupil is doing badly in school work, which depends considerably on reading and vocabulary; he is then given a mental ability test, replete with vocabulary and reading, and it is found that his IQ is consistent with his reading level. Therefore the conclusion is reached that the boy cannot read *because* he is dull. While the school makes an honest attempt to help him develop further, the conviction exists that the boy is doing as well as can be expected of one of his level of ability. Certainly by the time of entrance to junior high school, or even before, a much more sensible program for development of this youngster could be adopted if this process were recognized as circular reasoning and an effort made to break out of the circle.

In some cases further study of the pupil will result in a firm decision that his verbal abilities are genuinely low and that his reading achievement will probably remain quite modest—but that other assets can be cultivated so as to start him off toward a career requiring less of the aptitudes in which he is deficient and more of the aptitudes in which he is more adequate. On the other hand, if this further analysis indicates that the verbal ability rating of the youngster is primarily a reflection of his long years of reading disability, the causes of the reading disability become a matter of concern. The difficulty may be of emotional origin rather than lack of learning ability. Or, the disability may be due to ineffective work habits which can be modified even at this late date. The counselor's task then is to carry the pupil through the proper remedial program with reasonable hope that the verbal ability may improve when the specific handicap is removed.

Analyses of pupils' problems, of the type indicated in the last few sentences, are made much easier when we work with *multiple* measurement of *multiple abilities* rather than a "bushel basket" measurement of "intelligence." It is our belief, incidentally, that the same kind of differential measurement needs eventually to be extended further down the educational ladder than the late eighth or early ninth grade levels at which the *Differential Aptitude Tests* are especially effective.

Let us hasten to add that sometimes both the educational achievements of the pupil and his whole profile of aptitude test scores are low *and consistent*, leading to the temptation to accept the latter as a confirmation of the former. Even in such cases the counselor will do well to consider the possibility that some external factor has exerted a generally depressing effect. Clues may exist in the health record or in reports of home visits and conferences with parent. If, however, no history of glandular disorder, sensory defect, restricted cultural opportunity, or disparity of intellect with parents or siblings emerges, it is highly probable that the record is an accurate depiction of the individual.

The elementary principle is clear: the counselor must study the whole record. The tests and the achievement record do not make explicit the causal relationship; they are only data. Diagnoses must be made by the counselor, with a comprehensive, detective-like approach to determination of the possible causes. Several examples are presented in this booklet in which the counselors and the authors suspect or believe that the recorded ability profile is distorted by the present physical or emotional state of the person. In such cases, judgment regarding the potential ability of the person must be suspended and plans should be made for reappraisal after the underlying problems have been cared for.

In an ideal program, differentiated measurement of aptitudes paralleling differential measurement of achievements will constitute a sound starting point for the insightful appraisal of each youngster whose performance is not up to his measured abilities or the expectations of teachers, parents, and others.

What About the Flat Profile?

One of the most interesting experiences of the authors of the *Differential Aptitude Tests* was that the very name of the battery caused some counselors to expect every profile to have peaks and valleys and to expect consequently an obvious and easy key to each youngster's strengths and weaknesses. From the very nature of things, of course, many profiles will be more or less flat; a few at a very high level, some at a modest level, and a few at a low level. There are profiles in which all the percentile ranks are above the ninetieth, and there are profiles

11

in which no rank exceeds the tenth percentile. If all the tests in a battery were very highly intercorrelated, *all* profiles would be approximately flat; and, as a matter of fact, only one test would have to be given. The lower the intercorrelations among the tests, the more frequently irregular profiles will occur; *but even with intercorrelations close to zero among the tests, some profiles will come out approximately flat.*

It is quite natural then that on any test battery some of the profiles will show an absence of sharp peaks and valleys. There are all kinds of variations of this, such as the profile with only one dip or one peak. There are others that will show high scores in certain groups of aptitudes like Verbal, Numerical, and Language Usage, with low scores on the rest, and vice versa.

Differential prediction obviously thrives on peaks and valleys in profiles, but the reader should be aware that a flat profile at a high level, a medium level, or a low level is also significant. It is just as important, psychologically, to know that a person is rather undifferentiated on the abilities measured by these tests as to say that he has some unique assets or liabilities.

When one is confronted with what is essentially a flat profile, counseling will usually be concerned with the *general level* of this profile. For example, several things can be said about a person with a profile showing all of the ratings between the 45th and 55th percentiles on national norms, that is, an average and undifferentiated profile. If we believe the testing was accurate and the student tried hard, we can say that this student probably is below the level of ability necessary to enter or succeed in most colleges. We can say of a boy with such a profile that his ability level is high enough so that he can probably profit from special training in some field of interest to him, that it is not inevitable for him to look forward to the life of an unskilled worker or general laborer. Girls with the same kind of profile may be well suited to many clerical or distributive or personal service jobs, and many of them can learn special skills. For both sexes the counselor should know the level of abilities in the community as compared with national norms and the ability requirements for various local jobs. Thus counseling is profitable from a flat profile if one understands the meaning of the elements in the profile and has experience with the general requirements for occupations and levels of education.

Testing at Important Choice Points

In some cases in this booklet it is apparent that problems which were discovered in the upper grades could have been observed and treated much earlier. As modern school systems are organized, the junior high school years are crucial from the point of view of preventive counseling. A thorough investigation of strengths and weaknesses should occur at this point, when it is presumed that the youngster has mastered his fundamental skills and is about to enter upon a more differentiated educational program.

While the transitional years, grades eight and nine, are generally critical, it is evident that test-based counseling may be necessary for some pupils at almost any time. Programs must be changed, because of errors of judgment, changed interests, or shifts in the functional level of abilities with changes in motivation or in health. Occasionally socioeconomic shifts force changes in plans. Some pupils go along the college preparatory path with a modest record—only to find out late in high school that college entrance is blocked or that their desires for an academic career are less intense. Reconsideration of their career plans may call for a reappraisal, by test and otherwise, of their abilities.

Pre-college Counseling in Grade 12

The use of the *Differential Aptitude Tests,* or a similar battery, in the twelfth grade for the counseling of college preparatory students deserves special comment. A considerable number of twelfth-grade students who are planning to enter college are fairly certain of their educational plans. Many of them know exactly which colleges they want to enter and what alternatives they will accept if necessary. Many are quite sure of the general field for which they expect to prepare, such as engineering, business administration, teacher education, biological sciences, etc. But there are also appreciable numbers of rather competent twelfth-grade students who have not as yet settled on a specific objective. These students hope that the first year or two in college will provide an opportunity for exploration from which will emerge an area deserving of their concentration.

While it is true that many colleges provide a counseling service for their students, it is seldom that the freshman can have access to such counseling services prior to his admission or during the registration week. Of course, in some colleges the curriculum for the first year is inflexible, but most students will have some choice among several programs or a few subjects within a program. Some colleges will offer a diversified list of courses from which students must make their first-semester selections. Whatever the high schools can do to prepare students for wise choices of their first courses is all to the good.

Some college advisors will say that high school counselors often lack detailed knowledge of the requirements and opportunities in individual universities. It is granted that the pre-college counseling necessarily will be incomplete and that many details will need to be added at the time of the student's arrival on the campus. The fact is, however, that the high school counselor has a more thorough knowledge of the student at this stage than the college counselor can acquire during the first few days of the school year. Under these circumstances, if the high school senior can be given sufficient understanding of his own pattern of abilities and interests and a reasonable picture of the content of various courses, his freshman program can be chosen with a greater degree of discretion than would otherwise be the case.

The student of generally superior abilities who has not yet made a firm choice of a career can be encouraged to investigate several rather different areas during his first year and should enter the type of institution which makes this exploration possible. He should be advised of the necessity of appraising this broad educational experience so that he may later select an area of concentration that is both intellectually satisfying and appropriate from a career standpoint. It is often possible to elect a series of freshman courses which will be equally pertinent to several different majors. We are reminded of the high school senior who was debating whether he should enter an engineering program, a general program in the physical sciences, or a teacher education program in the sciences. The counselor helped him to enter a university which had a general freshman year leading to formal admission to the engineering college or transfer to the bachelor of science program with ease.

Sometimes a student without a clear pattern of interests may have an irregular profile of abilities. In such a case he should be encouraged to take a majority of courses suited to his aptitudes and be warned of the potential difficulties in those areas where his abilities are least. He should be advised of the existence of remedial courses where such are provided. He should not be encouraged to undertake a large amount of work in fields that will require excessive application to compensate for ineptitude. It is necessary to remember that many college failures occur during the freshman year, and that a successful and satisfying first semester can have an important bearing on a student's ultimate completion of college.

Interests and Aptitudes

In several of the cases presented here, scores from the *Kuder Preference Record* or the *Strong Vocational Interest Blank* are given. The counselors' reports do not indicate very adequately how these have affected the counseling. Presumably the scores have been integrated with other pertinent information.

Research studies published in educational and psychological journals reveal the relative independence of abilities and interests as tested by the *Strong* and the *Kuder* inventories. The evidence is clear that aptitude test scores and interest ratings are correlated only to a very small degree.[4]

Information with regard to the validity of interest inventories, especially for prediction of secondary school success, is meager. What there is suggests that seemingly relevant interest scores correlate less well with achievement records than do aptitude test scores. At best, interest scores have been shown to be only moderately correlated with achievement in a few fields of endeavor; as predictors of academic success, they are not as effective as aptitude tests. Super's summary of this matter is good background material to supplement the materials presented in the inventory manuals; Darley's excellent little book may also be helpful.[5]

Unfortunately, even in recent years, we have heard of counselors treating interest test scores as though they were measures of aptitude and considering the interest inventories and aptitude tests as convenient alternates. There is no excuse for this.

Because of the low intercorrelations of aptitude and interest indices, the counselor necessarily will be faced with discrepancies in ratings on aptitudes and interest which, logically, should "go together." Perhaps this statement can be a general guide: Use interest inventories to stimulate wider exploration of career possibilities and use aptitude tests and achievement records as predictors of the probable level of success in those aspects of the careers which depend on academic and special abilities.

Tests May Yield Critical Data, But "Logical" Action Does Not Ensue

There are situations in which test information is ignored even though we know that the data should be seriously considered in the decision.

---

[4]For one Grade 10 group, the 144 coefficients of correlation between the eight *DAT* scores and the nine *Kuder* scores, computed separately for boys and girls, were distributed as follows: An equal number were positive and negative; 95 of the 144 r's were between $\pm$ .20, and only 6 were over $\pm$ .40.

[5]Super, Donald E. *Appraising Vocational Fitness.* New York: Harper and Bros., 1949. Darley, John G. *Clinical Aspects and Interpretation of the Strong Vocational Interest Blank.* New York: The Psychological Corporation, 1941.

The reader will recall situations in which rigidity of thinking on the part of the family or of the pupil is so great or their level of aspiration is so high that, regardless of what facts we have, they persist in an inappropriate course of action.

The counselor is especially challenged in cases like these. He knows that certain objective facts, including test data, are relevant to the case and his big job is to bring the parents and counselee to a point where their decisions reflect the abilities indicated by the test scores.

The counselor, furthermore, can well be humble because the imperfect validity of both the instruments and the case-study method do not permit perfect predictions, and because a small percentage of highly motivated and well-organized pupils will succeed in spite of logical expectations of failure or low achievement. It is a rare counselor and a rarer school which does not have at least one prize example of the presumed sow's ear becoming the silk purse. The converse — a brilliant child ending up as a failure — is common enough to have generated a stereotyped belief that genius burns itself out.

There are several cases in this book which illustrate the satisfactory downward revision of a pupil's or a family's ambitions, and others in which the "logical" results of counseling were not acceptable. In still others we see just the beginnings of movement in the direction of more modest plans; in fact, the counselors were interested in bringing about gradual readjustment rather than a sudden reorganization of the person's self-concepts.

In contrast with these situations which involve lowering of aspirations, there are cases in which the counselor has used test data to raise the ambitions and working level of the counselee. In some instances the results were happy; in others the students persisted in serious underachievement. Logically if one "knows" his abilities he should be interested in performing at the corresponding levels. But often enough the under-achievement or lack of confidence in ability persists. In such cases the tests have been diagnostically useful, but further exploration of the emotional or social causes of failure is called for. This problem is discussed further in the last few pages of this introduction.

Then, there are the situations in which the socio-economic condition in the pupil's family or community is such that the counselee cannot carry out decisions which would seem otherwise reasonable and would be acceptable in the light of the test-based counseling. Fortunately, with our modern notions of public education and with our feeling of responsibility for the development of talent wherever we find it, this problem is becoming less frequent. Still, most counselors occasionally have the painful experience that their counseling goals must be modified because of seemingly invincible socio-economic barriers.

Challenging the Community

When it appears that some counselees cannot carry out lines of action proposed as sensible for them, the objective analysis of abilities can sometimes become the basis for advocating changes in the educational practices of the community or for seeking out special help for unusually talented pupils. In this lies one of the thrills of counseling, the satisfaction which comes from finding a youngster of previously unrecognized special talent and bringing success within his reach by using test scores and other facts to convince someone in the school system or community to give him the chance he needs.

To be sure, the philanthropists usually stress some vague concepts of strength of character or the worthiness of the applicant for aid. Granted that aid should go to those who are also most deserving from the point of view of character, it nevertheless remains that the discovery of talent warranting philanthropic (or governmental) assistance can be aided by objective measures, such as those in school records and in aptitude tests.

The above paragraphs stress the highly talented. The counselor should feel a rich satisfaction also when he has found patterns of career preparation for the less gifted pupils and when he has helped the community think through its needs for educational facilities for these pupils.[6]

Aptitude Test Scores as Signal Flags for Personality Maladjustment

In dealing with what seems to be primarily an educational and vocational problem, the counselor analyzes a set of aptitude test scores and related achievement records. Incongruities in the data sometimes appear which at first glance may cause him to question the value of tests because they just do not seem to work in the particular case. However, it does not necessarily follow that ignoring the test results is the right approach whenever test data are inconsistent.

To illustrate from a case which is not presented in this book, consider the situation of Amy, who tested around the 50th percentile on most of the *Differential Aptitude Tests*. An earlier test yielded an IQ around 100. This case was called to the attention of one of the editors by a

---

[6]Seashore, Harold G. Human resources and the aptitude inventory. *Test Service Bulletin* (The Psychological Corporation), No. 41, May 1951, 1-8.

school counselor who was asked to dig out from her records any cases on which tests "just didn't make sense." The school counselor reported that Amy was doing A and B work consistently in her third year in junior high school, and was carrying the regular curricular load. Amy was a so-called over-achiever.[7]

The author conferring with this counselor either had to agree that the tests did not reflect the girl's abilities or to suggest that there was something else in the situation which had not yet been considered. He began to ask some questions of the counselor. *What else did Amy do in school?* Practically nothing, because her mother supervised her so closely before and after school, and because Amy was so intent on sticking to her books. *What is her mother like?* Divorced, and having only one child, she is trying to compensate for her own disappointment in life through Amy; is determined to make her daughter self-sustaining and independent. *What about Amy's "personality"? Is she shy or gay? Does she participate socially?* Amy is very shy and often appears to be on the verge of crying. She is frequently fatigued and more than the usual amount of illness appears in her records. *Are there any signs of nervousness?* No, but—come to think of it—maybe that's not right because the school nurse and others have reported that Amy bites her nails, seems jittery at times, and is overly tense. In answering these probing questions, the counselor came to realize that Amy was probably pushing herself to the limits of her scholastic ability at an appreciable cost in health, to personality and in social adjustment. Some form of breakdown may occur unless Amy, and her mother too, are helped by someone skilled in mental hygiene. Or, Amy may just go on doing fairly well in an unhappy sort of way.

Serious discrepancies among test data themselves or in the relation of test data to other educational and personal information can also become important clues for discovery of the under-achiever, the youngster of much capacity whose attainment is not consistent with his abilities. Counselors generally agree that just telling such cases to "go to work" or "get on the ball" or "think of your future" is not very motivating. We are more and more convinced that deep-seated changes in the motiva-

---

[7]By over-achievement we mean simply that a student is performing better than we would have predicted. Our predictions can never be perfectly accurate—because no test battery is perfectly reliable or valid; because teachers' grades are usually even less reliable than tests; and because teachers' grades include judgments of work habits, promptness, diligence and other traits not measured by the tests. Our errors in prediction inevitably include underestimating the probable achievement of some pupils—who thus become "over-achievers."

Thus the "over-achiever" is not really working beyond his theoretical potentialities—he is one whose potentialities have been misjudged.

tional structure of the person or in his social environment are required.

In addition to the cases of discrepancy between expected and actual achievement, there are other kinds of situations in which aptitude test scores must be interpreted very cautiously, with careful regard for personality adjustments. For some of the cases in this booklet the editors have recommended that judgment be suspended until certain changes in the life of the person have occurred. There is, for example, the very obese girl with a consistent record of relatively low aptitude and relatively low achievement. The counselor discovered considerable emotional concern on the part of this girl with regard to her physical condition. Since she previously had tested somewhat higher in ability, there is reason to suspect that neither her achievement nor the aptitude profile necessarily depict her potentialities correctly. Of course, these are descriptions of her functioning in the current situation, but counseling requires predictions of her abilities at later stages under different, perhaps better, conditions.

Then there are the youngsters who already are known to the school as coming from very difficult or disorganized family situations and who are more appropriately subjects for a mental hygiene clinic than for the usual type of student counseling program. If the school counselor is not equipped to handle these deep-rooted problems, the best he can do is to seek help from outside agencies and to hold in abeyance judgments about the meaning of test scores or achievement records secured during this period.

No Separation of Educational, Vocational, and Personal Counseling

As we have been editing these case reports, we have become even more convinced that educational and vocational counseling can no longer properly be considered as independent of personal counseling. Counselors not only need to know the curriculum, psychometrics, and the requirements of various careers, but they must also understand the psychodynamics of human behavior. They need to develop insight and the ability to integrate all forms of case information into an understanding of the behavior and potentialities of the child. We do not mean that the counselor needs to be skilled in all aspects of clinical therapy and remedial education; but he does need to know what these are about, and to be familiar with the resources for referral. He must also be thoroughly aware that even though he has a heavy load of counseling, some of his cases will need repeated conferences for the slow transformation of personality and the development of insights. Many of the situations will be cleared up quickly in one or two short conferences; but if he fails to understand the clinical implications of some of his information, he may in other cases do more harm with these short conferences than if he had stayed out of the picture altogether.

Among the several competences demanded of the counselor who wishes to take a fully psychological approach to his work is that he be sophisticated in the general field of psychological measurement and understand thoroughly the strengths and weaknesses of the test batteries that he uses most frequently in his school. When well versed in test theory and practice, the counselor can use the test scores and ratings as significant contributors to the clinical aspects of his work.

Grade 12
Cases

Mary Dale

Problem: Mary sought help in her planning for higher education, after having had to give up her ambition to study medicine.

Tests

Differential Aptitude Tests. Grade 9.
An IQ of 111 was reported; test name and date of testing not given.

Report of Counseling in Grade 12

Mary has a relatively good achievement record. She was undecided about her plans for college. Her initial goal had been to become a doctor. Because of the inability of her family to contribute financially to her college training, it was necessary for Mary to try for a scholarship. She failed in this competition.

Mary was assisted in understanding herself a little better through discussion of her *Differential Aptitude Test* results with her counselor. It is apparent from her tests that she does not have the superior aptitudes required of students who are awarded scholarships to prepare for medical training. She is now working, and intends, after a year, to enter either a laboratory technician's school or a medical secretarial school. In view of her persisting interests, her present plans seem more realistic. The test profile suggests adequate ability for either the technician course or the secretarial course — except that, for the former, a higher Mechanical Reasoning score might be desirable and, for the latter, her Clerical Speed and Accuracy and Spelling ratings are a bit low.

Comments

The *Differential Aptitude Test* profile shows that Mary probably could enter a not-too-demanding college and do creditable work. Her present plans, however, seem to offer reasonable ways for her to satisfy her medical interests. Counseling should always take into account the motive behind the original choice of a goal; if Mary's desire to be a doctor reflected a concern for helping people, perhaps she would be happier as a social worker connected with a hospital, or as a nurse. If her interests are primarily technical, then her present plans are probably wiser. Merely scaling the ambitions downward is not enough; positive suggestions for exploring alternates which are consistent with interests and abilities are just as necessary parts of a sound counseling process.

The foregoing comments refer to Mary's vocational plan. It should also be pointed out that a girl of Mary's abilities might find one, two,

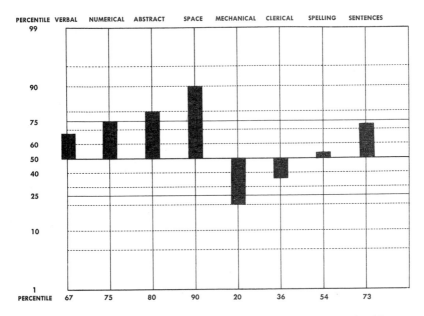

PERCENTILE	VERBAL	NUMERICAL	ABSTRACT	SPACE	MECHANICAL	CLERICAL	SPELLING	SENTENCES
PERCENTILE	67	75	80	90	20	36	54	73

or four years of liberal arts or general education to be a valuable experience apart from vocational preparation. As a matter of fact, her
vocational plan can be nicely integrated with a program in general
education in either junior college or in a regular, though not-too-demanding, liberal arts college. Counseling problems are so often expressed in
terms of vocational needs of young people that counselors sometimes
forget the important values of education for citizenship and for developing mature cultural interests.

Dorothy Hart

Problem: Dorothy wanted to crystallize her plans for college and a career.

Tests

Differential Aptitude Tests. Grade 12.
ACE Psychological Examination, High School. Grade 12. Percentile ranks: L-90, Q-71, Total-88.
Kuder Preference Record, Vocational. Grade 12. Percentile ranks: Outdoor — 77, Mechanical — 97, Computational — 48, Scientific — 89, Persuasive — 37, Artistic — 85, Literary — 11, Musical — 38, Social Service — 24, Clerical — 10.

Report of Counseling in Grade 12

Dorothy entered this year from a small high school. Her parents have some college background. She has five brothers. Poised, self-assured and friendly, Dorothy sought vocational counseling because she felt the need of a definite plan in view of the costs of higher education. She expressed interest in mathematics and science and was tentatively thinking of nursing as a career. Her academic record has been excellent, but at the time of first counseling she was concerned over her C grades in trigonometry and solid geometry. She felt that her merely average interest ratings in the computational areas stemmed from conflict with her teachers, although she also wondered whether she was graded too easily in the other school and really did not have the needed ability.

Test scores and grades would indicate enough academic strength to succeed in almost any area. A college program in mathematics and science was outlined which would still allow her some flexibility in choosing a major in the second half of college.

The *Differential Aptitude Test* scores and *Kuder Preference Record* ratings spurred her to consider the following fields: chemical engineering, laboratory technician, pathologist, statistician, actuary, economist.

Work experience in the statistical department of an insurance company was arranged. The personnel department indicated that Dorothy "knocked the top off our tests and is doing a superlative job . . . will be given more responsibility immediately and will be asked to continue during college and summers."

Dorothy says she is not interested in routine mathematics, but that research, perhaps in statistics or economics, holds a challenge.

The *DAT* scores, particularly Numerical and Abstract, did a great

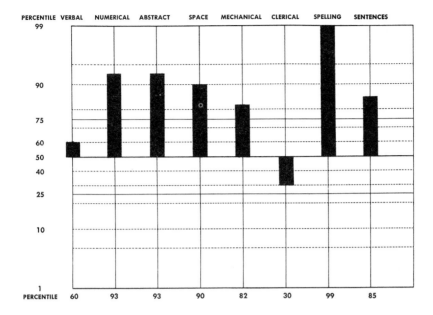

PERCENTILE	VERBAL	NUMERICAL	ABSTRACT	SPACE	MECHANICAL	CLERICAL	SPELLING	SENTENCES
PERCENTILE	60	93	93	90	82	30	99	85

deal to overcome her concern about her current progress in the two mathematics courses. She says she is "fascinated by the things figures can do — particularly in forecasting."

Comments

This case seems to represent a solid job of career thinking on the part of a bright girl entering a larger school, conscientious about her planning (with five boys in the family needing an education, too), and concerned about her momentarily below-average grades. The counselor used test data and interest ratings to assure her of her abilities, to guide her in a long-range program, and to direct her toward work-experiences which would be reassuring and stimulating. Even if Dorothy returns to her first tentative plan — a nursing career — the counseling process and the occupational explorations will have been helpful.

Dorothy's relative difficulties with mathematics, in the light of her test scores, suggest that the mathematics teacher, not Dorothy, may be the problem case! It is to be hoped that counselors are competent to analyze the educational process itself, as well as the pupils in it, and that an atmosphere of direct and friendly communication with both the school administration and the teachers is always maintained.

Ellsworth Newcomb

Problem: Ellsworth wanted help in changing his career plans, since his low mathematics grades caused him to question his plans for engineering.

Tests

Differential Aptitude Tests. Grade 12.

An *Otis* test. Grade 12. IQ-120.

Ohio State University Psychological Examination. Grade 12. 69th percentile on college freshman norms.

Kuder Preference Record. Grade 12. Highest areas: Literary, Persuasive, Social Service; low areas: Mathematics, Science. (Actual scores not reported.)

Strong Vocational Interest Blank. Grade 12. A ratings: Social Science Teacher, Personnel Manager, Public Administrator, and three sales fields.

Report of Counseling in Grade 12

Ellsworth's engineering aspirations had arisen in part from advice given him by a local industrialist. His mathematics grades were A, D, C, and C, indicating difficulty with a subject crucial to engineering. His work experiences had been in selling; he had found this work pleasant and had done well at it. When Ellsworth and his parents reviewed the whole situation, Ellsworth decided to drop his plans for engineering and prepare for business administration. His low Clerical rating was observed but was not considered crucial to the decision. His high verbal ability and language skills, his successful work experience, and his personal qualities argued for this choice. He was later graduated in the second fifth of his class, and he is now in college.

Comments

Open-minded parents can be persuaded by facts — facts from achievement records, from work experiences, from job descriptions, from interest questionnaires, and from aptitude test results. In this case the data added up to a consistent pattern which suggested college-level training but not in engineering. Whether he should study business administration or should complete a general liberal arts course with a social science or language major would be a matter of choice. If he had not wanted to go to college, on-the-job learning in industry or business

26

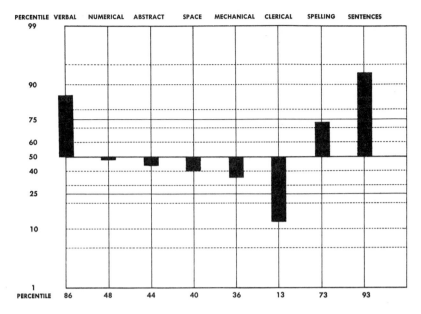

PERCENTILE	VERBAL	NUMERICAL	ABSTRACT	SPACE	MECHANICAL	CLERICAL	SPELLING	SENTENCES
PERCENTILE	86	48	44	40	36	13	73	93

(perhaps in selling) would have been consonant with his abilities and interests.

One cannot help remarking that while well-meaning, successful persons in the community can be helpful to the school counselor, they sometimes may mislead young people because of their halo as advisers. Most counselors like to enlist the aid of local business and professional men, but the wise choice of such volunteers is not easy. The self-chosen vocational counselor can present embarrassing problems.

Ellsworth solved his problem neatly, partly because of the detailed information yielded by the *Differential Aptitude Tests*. Like the *DAT* Verbal and Language Usage scores, the *OSU* rating indicated college ability. Useful as such a single-score test can be, the *DAT* and interest test profiles were much more specific in providing a basis for choosing among possible college opportunities.

Walter Zordaky

Problem: Walter had to face the fact that his plans for an engineering career were unrealistic.

Tests

Differential Aptitude Tests. Grade 12.
Henmon-Nelson. Grade 4. IQ-94.
California Mental Maturity. Grade 8. IQ-114. Also, Grade 10. IQ-102; L-104, NL-96.
California Progressive Achievement. Grade 8. Grade equivalents: Reading — 7.9, Vocabulary — 5.9, Arithmetic Comprehension — 8.8, Arithmetic Reasoning — 7.1, English — 5.9, Spelling — 5.5.
SRA Reading Record. Grade 10. Percentile rank-9.
Kuder Preference Record, Vocational. Grade 11. Percentile ranks: Outdoor—30, Mechanical—87, Computational—93, Scientific—70, Persuasive—35, Artistic—28, Literary—3, Musical—30, Social Service —47, Clerical—79.
ACE Psychological Examination, High School. Grade 12. Percentile ranks: L-8, Q-55, Total-15.

Report of Counseling in Grade 12

Walter is the elder of two sons of an immigrant father who has developed a large and profitable structural steel business. A younger brother in Grade 8 is doing well. There is no noticeable conflict between the brothers.

In Grade 9 Walter earned B's and C's in his courses, which included practical mathematics and general shop. In Grades 10, 11 and 12 he had C's and D's in academic courses and B's in shop and mechanical drawing. In Grade 12, he earned B and C in his *repeat* terms of geometry. He had dropped Spanish and had taken no sciences. His program did not meet college entrance requirements either in quality or in coverage.

His father has occasion to work with engineers and his plans for his son have always included engineering. He wants Walter to have professional status even though the business does not necessarily require that type of training. The counselor visited the plant and spent a half day watching all operations; the job includes some design skill but mostly requires blueprint reading and layout work. Walter has worked in the plant, has designed forms and jigs, and seems well versed in plant knowledge and skills. He, too, wants engineering, but has obviously avoided sciences and language and has not been very successful in mathematics.

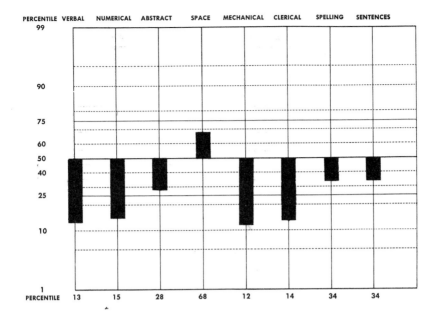

PERCENTILE	VERBAL	NUMERICAL	ABSTRACT	SPACE	MECHANICAL	CLERICAL	SPELLING	SENTENCES
PERCENTILE	13	15	28	68	12	14	34	34

His father's status drive does not seem to be affected by counseling; he is completely adamant about Walter's studying to be an engineer.

The counselor feels that the test results indicate probable failure for Walter in a four-year engineering program, but that a two-year program tailored to fit Walter's needs might be feasible. However, planning is stymied because anything short of a regular program is unacceptable to the father.

Walter is now writing to preparatory schools about further training. In the counselor's opinion, counseling should be directed toward preparation for possible failure. It is expected that the father sooner or later will say something like ". . . our firstborn son, for whom we have sacrificed everything, and now you let us down this way . . ."

Comments

The counselor began using the *DAT* battery in this school during Walter's last year. The profile served as a corroboration of earlier evidence of ability not consistent with the father's ambitions for his son. The *California Mental Maturity Test* IQs in Grade 10, while average, did not indicate college ability. We wonder why the counselor did not give the alternate form of the Mechanical Reasoning test since the low rating (12) does not seem quite what one would expect from his record. Counseling can be more confidently pursued if discrepancies between test data and other data are taken as challenges to secure more facts. We note also that the Space score is consistent with his success in mechanical drawing, shop and geometry (as repeated).

The counselor does not report much about Walter's own deeply felt needs; the implication is that he would settle for a more realistic plan. That he was a dutiful son is also evident. Walter has shown that he can learn "on the job." Whatever strengths he showed in school were directly related to work in his father's plant. If he really needs some further technical training not best secured by an apprenticeship, Walter could well pursue the plan for a two-year technical program which has been proposed.

Perhaps the family's ideas of status and job requirements will be reorganized the hard way. Walter, at the time of reporting, was attempting to enter a preparatory school to bolster his record for college. He must first be admitted to the preparatory school, then pass his course, and then be accepted by an engineering college. There are years of rough going ahead — and the probability is that he will fail to achieve his father's objective. The internal evidence does not indicate that his difficulties are due to sociocultural limits of an immigrant home or to lack of his trying to do school work well. We must, of course, be aware of the unlikely possibility that Walter may start "clicking."

On the other hand, so sure is the counselor that Walter will fail in his four-year engineering plan (either by not being admitted or by failure in the course), that he has pointed the counseling toward protecting the school and toward softening for the boy the consequences of his father's final realization of the facts in the situation.

The serious counselor cannot separate his educational-vocational advice from the total situation — a point well illustrated by the case of Walter, whose father's emotionalized goals are the major obstacle to a reasonable life plan.

Grade 11
Cases

Sarah Carrell

Problem: Sarah's mother wanted her to withdraw from school before Sarah could complete the commercial course.

Tests

Differential Aptitude Tests. Grades 9 and 10.
Otis Classification. Grade 8. Percentile rank—47.
Cooperative Reading Comprehension. Grade 9. Percentile ranks: Vocabulary — 50, Speed — 53, Level — 66, Total — 58.

Report of Counseling in Grade 11

Early in her junior year, Sarah talked over her test scores with the counselor. Her school work had been satisfactory. She then appealed for help in persuading her mother that it was worth while to finish high school. The mother wished her to go to work since her father had just been forced to retire on a small pension. The mother felt Sarah was over-age (illness in childhood had retarded her one year), and that she would not do well in secretarial training because her school grades were not above average. Moreover, none of Sarah's older brothers and sisters had graduated from high school and the mother considered high school of little value for a girl.

The mother finally agreed to come to school for a conference. The counselor pointed out that while Sarah's *Differential Aptitude Test* scores were low in Spelling and Sentences, she had above average scores in Numerical and Abstract and her clerical aptitude was average. Sarah could learn calculating skills and bookkeeping and could continue her typing if she remained in school. The mother then admitted that her secret desire had been for Sarah to work in an insurance office where her brother-in-law could secure her a job. She conceded that if Sarah was that good, she ought to have a chance to finish school. With the fear of having to leave school no longer haunting her, Sarah has settled down to work harder than she had previously in her school career, especially on her language skills.

Comments

One of the American ideals is that every child should be educated in a way that will challenge his abilities and permit him to serve society well regardless of his socio-economic origins. Sarah's family had low career expectancies for its members. At a time of crisis — her father's lessened income — it seemed natural to change Sarah from a dependent pupil to an income-producer. With her abilities Sarah probably could

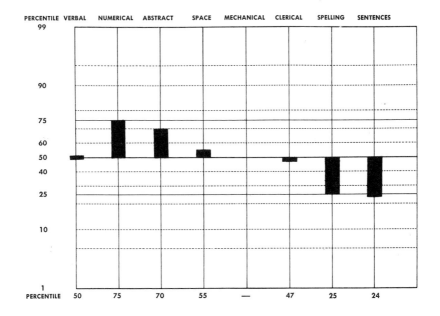

PERCENTILE	VERBAL	NUMERICAL	ABSTRACT	SPACE	MECHANICAL	CLERICAL	SPELLING	SENTENCES
PERCENTILE	50	75	70	55	—	47	25	24

attain eventually a fairly good weekly wage; for many well-paying jobs the extra years in school might not even make a contribution. A two-year delay in earnings could seem unreasonable.

Apparently the counselor succeeded in helping the mother accept a delay in Sarah's earning in favor of better training in a field which was appropriate to her and which was secretly valued by the mother.

We are not told how the family was to get along without her earnings. Maybe there were other resources, maybe part-time work was secured, maybe the family felt the sacrifice worth while. Counselors need to be aware of the intricacies of counseling when economic difficulties are involved. Acceptance of Sarah's plan by her mother was logical and reasonable *if* it was true that the family could afford a delay in her contribution. Suppose they could not—or felt they could not! Having stirred up new ambitions in Sarah, what kind of counseling would be needed? Suppose the mother was adamant about taking the pupil out? How far should the counselor enter into a family controversy?

Matching a pupil's abilities with a curriculum or career plan on the basis of previous achievement, a profile of test scores, and expressed interests is the easiest part of counseling. More difficult, but just as necessary, is the integration of these with such other considerations as social class, financial resources, and the beliefs and emotional patterns of the pupil, the family and influential friends. Counseling Sarah was partly a process of moving a girl across class boundaries; social mobility was occurring during these decision-making conferences.

Martin Cummings

Problem: Martin, with a rather poor record, is confronted with a choice of finishing his high school program or dropping out of school.

Tests

Differential Aptitude Tests. Grade 11.
Otis Q-S, Beta. Grade not given. IQ-102.

Report of Counseling in Grade 11

Martin is 18 and in Grade 11, having spent two years in Grade 10. He is in the commercial course and asked for a change to the general academic course. His father prefers that he leave school, but the son wants to earn a high school diploma.

Martin was shown that his profile indicated adequate abilities to carry the general course to which he wished to change. He decided to stay where he is. There is no improvement in his achievement and he has a high absence record. The father seems to be winning, if only by forcing his son out via the failure route.

Comments

The foregoing brief notes leave much to be desired in the way of information as to the counseling process and how these decisions emerged. We do not have enough background to permit us to trace Martin's low achievement to its causes. He apparently does not lack the abilities to do the work. Perhaps the commercial program is not a challenge to his interests; an interest inventory might supply some clues. With a record of failure, he probably is unwilling to try another course, traditionally considered more difficult.

We feel that this boy should not drop out with this record of failure. How much better it would be if, through counseling with both the father and the son, the father's cooperation could be enlisted so that Martin could end his school career with a diploma. Knowing this school, we can see some of the reasons why this better solution was not forthcoming: there are too few well-trained counselors, and too little opportunity to locate boys like Martin earlier.*

---

*Martin's school, for reasons which probably seem appropriate to its administrators, tests students when they become "problem cases." Other schools have found it desirable to test on a grade-wide basis at certain critical points (such as the eighth or ninth grade, or the eleventh grade) in order that the test data will be available promptly when problem cases arise. More importantly, this survey type of testing enables the counselors to compare ability patterns with achievement patterns of all members of the class and, by such a procedure, to anticipate crises before they arise. The argument is made that the survey type of testing of the whole class is too ex-

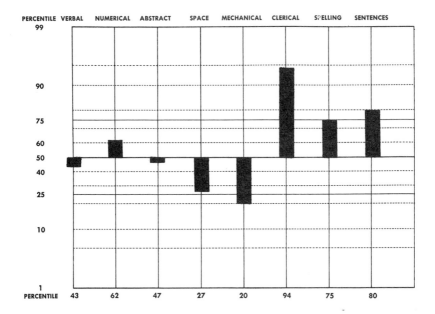

PERCENTILE	VERBAL	NUMERICAL	ABSTRACT	SPACE	MECHANICAL	CLERICAL	SPELLING	SENTENCES
PERCENTILE	43	62	47	27	20	94	75	80

Counseling *before* the crisis, instead of after the failure, would have been much more economical for all concerned. Martin needed this counseling at least as early as the first time he tried the tenth grade. We estimate that the school system has wasted at least five hundred dollars on his repeated year and the special attention he has required. And even this cost by no means matches the human cost in time and spirit.

If a counselor could handle a case load of only fifty serious cases a year and prevent such waste in a dozen or so, the financial saving alone to the community would be tremendous. Why is it that we expect industry to husband carefully its resources and its inventory of supplies, but are not very excited when human beings and educational budgets are wasted? Counseling cannot solve all such problems — but on a sheer dollars and cents basis a community cannot afford to be unconcerned about preventive counseling.

---

pensive because, it is pointed out, perhaps half or even fewer of the students will ever be counseled on a case basis. Furthermore, if counselors have to study the records of all the students in advance of their becoming problem cases, counseling costs go up.

There are several answers to this viewpoint. First, if the school feels that it has a real obligation to provide personalized counseling service to its students, it will necessarily counsel a considerable proportion of the students at some time during their secondary school careers. Second, since the counseling of serious problem cases is very expensive, any program of action whereby cases can be anticipated and handled before they become full-blown crises will be cheaper in the long run in terms of staff time, teacher involvement, administrative actions, and certainly in terms of time and strain on the student and his family. Preventive counseling usually will result in more students being seen for shorter periods of time than when the counselor becomes involved in the more prolonged process of counseling-in-crisis.

Betty East

Problem: Betty wanted to clarify her educational plans, which were complicated by personality problems related to her obesity.

Tests

Differential Aptitude Tests. Grade 11.

IQs-115; 129. Grade 9 or earlier. Parochial school report.

Wechsler-Bellevue. Grade 11. Full Scale IQ-117, Verbal IQ-113, Performance IQ-115.

Kuder Preference Record. Grade 11. Above 75th percentile in Computational, Literary, Social Service. Low in Scientific and Clerical. (Actual scores not reported.)

Report of Counseling in Grade 11

Betty requested counseling and asked for tests because one of her friends had taken them. Her planning seemed hazy; she thought she might like interior decorating, nursing or psychology. No reasons were given for her choices.

The nurse reports: "Obese girl; 100 pounds overweight; now receiving medication for thyroid difficulty; tendency to overeat; needs encouragement to stay on diet."

After a session during which the counselor described the test results, Betty talked of plans for college. Her goals seemed unrealistic in terms of both marks and finances. She expressed interest in social work, occupational therapy, police work, guidance counseling, personnel, and psychiatric social work. At the same time, she has little interest in her present school work and anticipates failing one subject (journalism). Another counseling session followed a period during which she read about the occupations noted above.

Betty feels she is "so big and fat." The doctor says she probably will be normal in weight by the time she graduates. She now says she really wants to enter the armed services, preferably the Marines. She feels she cannot think clearly about the future until she becomes more nearly normal in weight. She seemed very pleased that she had lost considerable weight already. She still shows no interest in passing her journalism course. Counseling is to be continued.

Comments

Obviously Betty's educational and career planning is complicated by her physical condition. It is good that both the physiological problem and the psychological problem of school adjustment are being met simultaneously. A better understanding by the staff and by Betty herself of

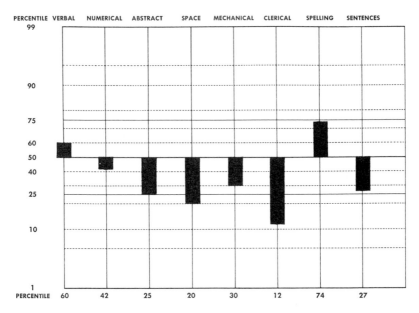

PERCENTILE	VERBAL	NUMERICAL	ABSTRACT	SPACE	MECHANICAL	CLERICAL	SPELLING	SENTENCES
PERCENTILE	60	42	25	20	30	12	74	27

her emotional reactions to her obesity and the possible ill effects of these feelings on her school work is needed. The counselor is forced to move only as fast as Betty's health improves and she becomes responsive to counseling. Betty is lowering her level of aspiration in the light of her school record and her counselor's interpretation of her aptitudes.

In making this report to us, the counselor calls attention to the discrepancy between the level of the *DAT* profile and IQs on earlier group testing (115 and 129), and on a more current *Wechsler-Bellevue* examination (117). Actually, the *Differential Aptitude Test* profile (Grade 11) is more consistent with her scholastic record than are the IQs. However, both the group test scores and her achievement may have been depressed by her emotional condition; if good rapport was established by the examiner, it is possible that the individually administered test was more accurate. Her marks in Grade 9 were numerically higher, but were earned at a different school where standards may have been different, so that evaluation of these marks is difficult. Such discrepancies, especially those between the concurrent *Wechsler-Bellevue* and *DAT* ratings, normally should lead (a) to checking up on the quality of test administration in the school and, (b) to retesting with alternate forms or with different tests.

The situation calls for suspended judgment. Betty is being given considerable supportive counseling now to help her through this difficult period of late adolescence during which physical unattractiveness can be such a crushing experience. As her condition — both physical and emotional — improves, a reappraisal of her abilities should be made.

Robert Finchley

Problem: Robert had a long record of poor achievement which seemed inconsistent with his family's status.

Tests

Differential Aptitude Tests. Grades 9 and 10.
Otis Classification. Grade 8. Percentile rank—55.
Cooperative Reading Comprehension. Grade 9. Percentile ranks: Vocabulary — 50, Speed — 24, Level — 32, Total — 32.

Report of Counseling in Grade 11

Robert presented a problem to teachers, parents and counselors ever since he entered ninth grade. His parents were college graduates and people of distinction in the community. His younger sister was superior in mental ability, school performance and social adjustment. Robert had been a somewhat precocious child but, as he advanced in school, his grades tended to fall below average. He developed a dislike for reading and for written work. By the time he entered high school he avoided preparation of any written assignments which would reveal his inadequacies. While Robert pretended to feel that spelling, keeping of notebooks, etc., were of no importance, the teachers and counselor felt that he was becoming certain that he was well below average mentally. His freshman classification test and reading test scores were not reassuring. Many of his teachers began to question his capacity. Although his counselor tried to help him realize that his general attitude and poor work habits, rather than lack of ability, were responsible for his difficulties, he remained unconvinced.

Although tested during the ninth and tenth grades, Robert was not scheduled for counseling until his junior year. His *Differential Aptitude Test* profile, with its evidence of some high aptitudes, delighted him. His teachers could see signs that this new self-confidence was influencing his attitude toward his work. His English teacher especially commented on his improvement. Robert himself for the first time admitted he could see he had been running away from his real problem. He became interested in investigating colleges, particularly schools of engineering. His teachers also felt that they now could help him more effectively.

Comments

Robert — presumed in elementary years to be bright — was regarded as of mediocre ability when in the ninth grade. A reading test and a scholastic ability test (loaded with reading) seemed to verify the

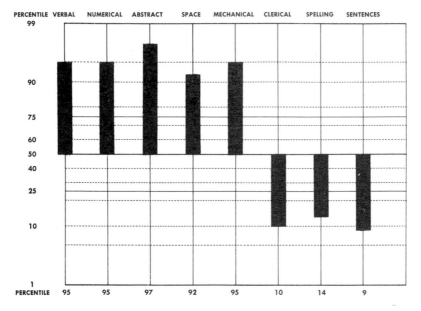

PERCENTILE	VERBAL	NUMERICAL	ABSTRACT	SPACE	MECHANICAL	CLERICAL	SPELLING	SENTENCES
PERCENTILE	95	95	97	92	95	10	14	9

growing judgment of the teachers and Robert himself that he really wasn't very able. If the *Differential Aptitude Tests* had been used two years previously, Robert might have had an earlier chance to reveal his abilities in a testing program which permits more or less discrete abilities to show themselves and which includes some tests which have relatively low reading requirements.

The low *Otis* and *Cooperative Reading* test results and the low Language Usage scores, for which both parts are out of line with the rest of his performance on the *DAT*, would have been signals calling for remedial attention to severe handicaps in important skills of an otherwise very bright boy.

Unfortunately the diagnosis was delayed until the beginning of Grade 11. Then the counseling sessions included discussion of the tests. This seemed (a) to release latent motivational forces in Robert and, (b) to induce more helpful responses among his teachers. They were talking now of his several abilities and his identified handicaps.

The specific remedial steps for bolstering his language usage deficiency were not reported. With his new motivation and his real abilities, he may "catch up" without much special retraining. Or it may turn out that this boost is only temporary and superficial in effect — real psychotherapy may be required before a permanent gain can occur. At any rate, the demands of the situation are now more clearly recognized.

Users of the "counseling from profiles" approach quickly realize that single-score scholastic aptitude tests, dependent on reading comprehension, may yield misleading descriptions of boys and girls.

Grace Spring

Problem: Grace was failing in the commercial program and wanted to discuss a change to another vocational program.

Tests

Differential Aptitude Tests. Grade 11.
Kuder Preference Record. Grade 11. High areas: Computational, Clerical and Social. (Actual scores not reported.)

Report of Counseling in Grade 11

Grace came to the counselor's attention because she was failing several subjects in the commercial program she had chosen. Although the *Kuder Preference Record* showed that her choice of program was in line with her interests as she recognized them, neither her program nor her interests matched her abilities very well. The counselor felt that her relatively high scores in Space Relations and Mechanical Reasoning, as compared with her poor-to-middling scores in the aptitudes pertinent to clerical or secretarial work, warranted some effort aimed at arousing new interests and altering her plans.

The result of the counseling sessions was that Grace requested transfer to the dressmaking course in the Vocational School. This request was honored, with good results in both achievement and attitude. She is doing good work in the shop courses and average work in the remainder of her classes. Her attendance has improved, and she now expects to qualify for a regular high school diploma.

Comments

A single IQ rating for this girl — or even a verbal-and-numerical or verbal-and-nonverbal comparison — would not have been sufficiently diagnostic. The aptitude basis for her plan to enter the dressmaking course could not have been adequately appraised. A decision based in part on analysis of her *Differential Aptitude Test* profile made good sense to her and to her counselor.

Fortunately in this case there was no evidence of parental objection to the change. Much too often the counselor's task is complicated by the need to help parents accept a transfer to a program which they feel, consciously or unconsciously, implies a lower social status. Other cases in this series reflect this problem, although the tendency to regard only the secretary, the nurse and the teacher as acceptable models for a girl's ambitions is happily decreasing. In the long run the counselor must

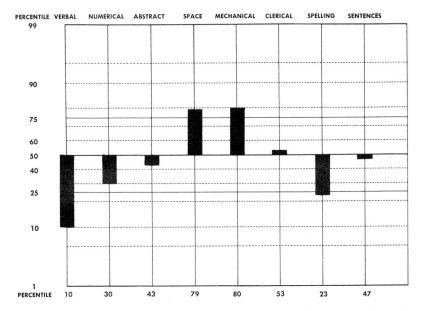

PERCENTILE	VERBAL	NUMERICAL	ABSTRACT	SPACE	MECHANICAL	CLERICAL	SPELLING	SENTENCES
PERCENTILE	10	30	43	79	80	53	23	47

share in helping the whole community accept the philosophy that all school programs are honorable and that educational and vocational decisions should be based on the genuine abilities of the child and not on notions of social hierarchy.

41

Ronald Trapp

Problem: Ronald, a failing student, has made a relatively unsuccessful attempt at improving his reading; on the basis of aptitude tests he was identified for the first time as a fairly capable boy whose reading disability and low verbal level might stem from deep-seated anxiety.

Tests

Differential Aptitude Tests. Grades 9 and 10.
A mental ability test in Grade 6. (CA 12-5) MA 8-3.
Stanford Achievement. Grade 6. Grade levels from 2.9 to 4.8 on the various parts.
Otis Classification. Grade 8. Percentile rank — 1.
Cooperative Reading Comprehension. Grade 9. Percentile ranks: Vocabulary—33, Speed—62, Level—22, Total—37.
Kuder Preference Record, Vocational. Grade 9. Percentile ranks: Mechanical — 47, Computational — 40, Scientific — 31, Persuasive — 86, Artistic — 84, Literary — 4, Musical — 55, Social Service — 70, Clerical — 60.
Kuder Preference Record, Personal. Grade 11. Percentile ranks: Sociable—9, Practical—47, Theoretical—70, Agreeable—75, Dominant — 43.

Report of Counseling in Grade 11 and Earlier

This case had been carried on for about two years at time of report and involved several staff members and agencies. Therefore a form of reporting different from that of other cases in this booklet is used.

Overview by Counselor, Fall 1950, Grade 11. This boy is now a junior in high school. His grades reveal a constant struggle to pass. In subjects where reading is involved, any grade above D probably has been given to him because of his effort.

Ronald is very level-headed, has good common sense, and is very dependable. He has suffered through his school years by being considered "dumb" by his schoolmates. In fact, I have heard rather cruel jokes at his expense. Some teachers have also felt that he was rather hopeless as far as learning was concerned. He has been in remedial reading classes almost constantly.

The *Differential Aptitude Tests* were administered partly in Grade 9A and partly in Grade 10A; Ronald was counseled during Grade 10. After making out the graph for this test I invited Ronald in. I asked

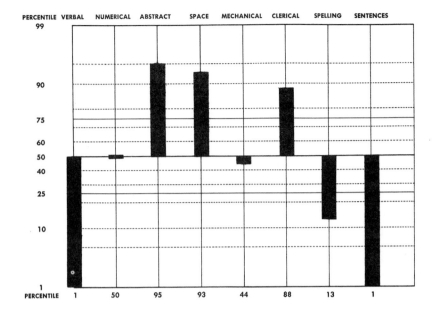

PERCENTILE	VERBAL	NUMERICAL	ABSTRACT	SPACE	MECHANICAL	CLERICAL	SPELLING	SENTENCES
PERCENTILE	1	50	95	93	44	88	13	1

him if he ever felt discouraged about his ability to learn and he, of course, replied that he did. The profile, I felt, was very significant in that it was the first tangible evidence we had to show him that he did have some outstanding abilities and what they were.

Together, we came to the conclusion that his reading deficiency was the cause of his school failures and that back of this there might be an emotional block. Our next step was to persuade him to seek help on his own accord from the Mental Hygiene Clinic.

Background information includes: English language used in home. Father ill in a state hospital. Mother remarried. Two brothers, ages 22 and 11. His grades in standard academic courses have all been D's or failure. His special courses are better: Shop (three years of A's and B's), Art (two years of B's), Gym and Safety (A's), Auto Mechanics (one year of C's), Business Arithmetic (C's).

Remedial Reading Program. In 1948, Grade 9, Ronald was referred for remedial reading work and all year he worked with a grade school reading specialist. At that time his reading level was Grade 1; during the year she brought him up to Grade 6 level. Recently he told her, "When you told me I could learn to read I thought you were kidding. Now the clinic tells me I can and now I think I can learn."

The Clinic Report. Although Ronald agreed to request an appointment at the local mental hygiene clinic during Grade 10, he was not able to become an active case until September of 1950, in Grade 11.

43

There are two long reports, one dated September 1950 and one, a summary, dated April 1951. Following are digests of these reports.

a. *Diagnostic examination, September 1950.*

Problem: Ronald was referred to the clinic by the schools because of his very poor reading. He is quite adequate in other areas and is well liked by teachers and classmates. He exhibited no behavior problems. A psychological examination is desired as an aid in determining the basis for his reading difficulty.

Test Results: The over-all rating on the *Wechsler-Bellevue* places Ronald in the range of average intelligence, but in particular areas he shows ability markedly above average. His performance was superior on those tasks involving spatial relationships and quantitative reasoning. In general he did better on nonverbal than verbal tasks. He did poorly on the information, vocabulary and similarities subtests. . . . Other clinical tests suggest an insecure, constricted individual with tendencies towards withdrawal . . . and inability to respond on a feeling level.

No evidence is seen of deviant or pathological thinking. Perception of reality is good. The record reflects much constriction and repression.

Summary: In the test situation Ronald's manner was compliant and cooperative, but quite unspontaneous. Test results show markedly uneven intellectual functioning and give no evidence of any organic basis for either this or his reading problems. The strong emotional conflicts present could account for this type of functioning. Although test results do not reveal the source of his problems, they do show a very repressed individual with much underlying hostility and anxiety. His rigid defenses and difficulty in relating to people on other than a superficial level make therapeutic prognosis questionable.

b. *Summary of Contacts and Findings, April 1951.*

Ronald was first seen in the clinic on September 27, 1950. He made his own contacts under the direction of his school counselor. The problem which he defined was one of reading difficulty. He presented a picture of many futile attempts at learning to read. There is a great deal of emotional upset regarding his father and the problems in the area of family relations. He said that he had been unfortunate because his father's illness prevented a companionable relationship.

The relationship with his older brother, aged 22, is quite close. Ronald is worried that his younger brother, 11, will have a reading problem like his own. His history shows headaches, used as a defense; also, an attack of rheumatic fever at 13 years of age caused him to remain in bed for several months.

The clinic study reveals that Ronald has a repressed, constricted personality with many strong defenses. Anxiety-cloaked hostility and rebellion are present deep beneath the surface. He has strong needs and many ego-alien wishes. At the same time, he has a need to deny the above feelings.

He is inclined to withdraw whenever he feels loss of control. He inhibits himself constantly. It should be noted that he has good ability in the quantitative area. It is significant that there is a 19-point difference between the *Wechsler-Bellevue* Verbal and Performance IQs.

It is his strong defenses which make it difficult to predict the effect of therapy. He had some difficulty in establishing a relationship with a male therapist. He related all of his problems to reading. However, as therapy has progressed (on a weekly basis) he has been able to accept the therapist; and, although he still feels threatened, there is some evidence that Ronald will be able to break through these defenses. Although therapy will be a long-drawn-out affair, his attitude toward it is such that he will undoubtedly continue for the benefits which he expects to derive. If therapy is successful and he can interact more genuinely with people, achieve a better understanding and have less feeing of hostility, the reading block will undoubtedly disappear.

What Several Teachers Say about Ronald, April 1951. Has a grade of D — partly out of courtesy, or shall we say common sense, I intend to pass him. He tries not as hard as he could — but harder than some. . . . Not a discipline problem—doesn't do much—he's terribly limited, as you know . . . Reading is so difficult for him that he fails all tests. If I read the questions to him and let him answer orally he does B work usually. His attitude is good. His effort is fair. He takes part in demonstrations and recitations — but doesn't put any effort into reading assignments. Relationship with teacher good — students tend to poke fun at him. Takes a serious attitude. . . . He is liked by all the fellows. Willingly enters into whatever I (the coach) suggest. He is always chosen among the first by the boys. Enters into the give and take of high school boys. Is social-minded, only being held back by the usual shyness. Loves to hunt and trap. . . . Elected a class officer last spring. I think Ronald feels certain inadequacies and having a prestige with students helps his sense of well-being. . . . Seemingly had no desire for high achievement in art. Wants to be of his group — but sought oblivion when it came to turning out a superior piece of work. He had a tendency to condescend smilingly to me (art instructor) when I complimented him on a particular piece of work.

Comments

This rather complete report has many ramifications. It is hard to see just *why* Ronald should have been unrecognized so long as a case calling for full treatment in a mental hygiene clinic. There may be many reasons. Among them is the fact that nobody seems to have seriously questioned Ronald's low mental ability rating. It happened that he had been measured by tests requiring the very skills he lacks, or the kinds of responses he is emotionally blocked from making. The first differential information came in Grade 9 — a percentile rank of 1 on the Verbal Reasoning test and ranks of 50 and 95 on Numerical Ability and Abstract Reasoning. Yet a year passed before these signal flags were acted on. During that year he did grow from Grade 1 to Grade 6 in reading competence — but the emotional origins of his difficulty were still not recognized. The remaining *DAT* scores secured in the spring of Grade 10 completed the picture — a rather bright boy, with low Verbal and Language Usage test scores. Note that we say test scores, not abilities. The chances are great that the scores were depressed by Ronald's emotional state; as therapy progresses, he may show very rapid changes in these abilities now rated so low. As of this report, we do not know whether or not his verbal ability has been seriously under-estimated.

We asked the counselor to retest Ronald in Grade 11 on Verbal Reasoning and Language Usage; his percentile ratings as of then were 7 for Verbal Reasoning, 3 for Spelling, and 1 for Sentences. Therapy had not resulted in measurable improvement by then.

The differential measurement of Ronald at Grade 8 or 9, with prompt *action* on the basis of the findings, might have brought Ronald to an appropriate rehabilitation program. Maybe late adolescence is too late. Two things are certain — testing with too limited instruments, mislabeled Ronald in Grade 6 and Grade 8, and the more informative testing begun in Grade 9 should have led to referral and clinical action *before* Grade 11.

With regard to the staff which presented this case, let it be said (a) that their program of special school services with an adequate testing program is new, (b) they used their own remedial facilities quite well and (c) it is not their fault that the local clinic has such a crowded schedule that new cases must wait almost a whole year before beginning therapy. Surely the psychologist and the counselors have in Ronald, and other Ronalds, some powerful arguments for more and better facil-ities for the early discovery and prompt handling of problem cases.

Grade 10
Cases

Kay Bacall

Problem: Kay, a girl of little ability and poor achievement, but with high family standards, was concerned about college and plans for entering nursing or elementary teaching.

Tests

Differential Aptitude Tests. Grade 11.

California Mental Maturity. Grade 9. IQ-93; L-103, NL-81.

Stanford Achievement. Grade 8 (8.2). Grade equivalents: Paragraph Meaning—9.1, Word Meaning—8.3, Language Usage—8.0, Spelling—7.0, Arithmetic Reasoning—9.3, Arithmetic Computation—10.3, Total—9.0.

Progressive Achievement. Grade 8. Corroborated the above.

Kuder Preference Record, Vocational. Grade 11. Percentile ranks: Outdoor—71, Mechanical—61, Computational—15, Scientific—13, Persuasive—75, Artistic—50, Literary—46, Musical—82, Social Service—97, Clerical—16.

Report of Counseling in Grades 10 and 11

Kay was seen several times, beginning in Grade 10, for course adjustments and career planning. Her long-time pattern has been one of slow learning. There is no simple explanation for the discrepancy between her above-grade achievement test results in arithmetic and a long record of trouble in arithmetic and more recently in algebra (a grade of D) and geometry (D, dropped); currently her practical mathematics grades have been B and C. Her interest in computational activities seems to be low. Her only other B's in high school have been in civics and problems of democracy. She dropped Latin and Spanish and received a D in French. She is now in the practical course, having recently abandoned the college preparatory program.

Her counseling sessions over the past two years have been with several counselors, and with each she has displayed highly emotional behavior whenever her wishes were not immediately gratified. Only after checking hospital requirements did she acknowledge that nursing was not realistic since she felt unable to cope with scientific or mathematical subjects. She then redirected her interest toward elementary school teaching. To this goal she has held steadfastly, being unable to accept interpretations of aptitude and achievement tests. She repeatedly comes back with, "But I want to work with children and have a college education."

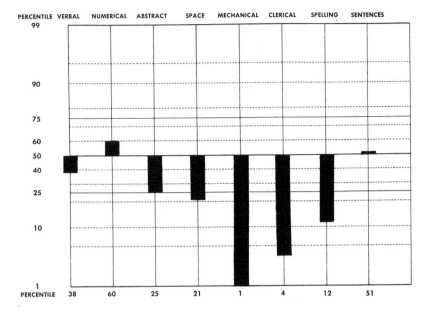

PERCENTILE	VERBAL	NUMERICAL	ABSTRACT	SPACE	MECHANICAL	CLERICAL	SPELLING	SENTENCES
PERCENTILE	38	60	25	21	1	4	12	51

The parents are cooperative and recognize the girl's limitations, but have not been able to help her seek more realistic goals. She is emotionally unstable and cries frequently. She does not appear to be accepted by her classmates, and compensates for this by almost compulsive participation in class discussions. Her elementary record further supports this pattern of emotional insecurity—"she does not make friends easily —is often on fringes socially, and apt to be a 'cry baby' when things go wrong."

Comments

Apart from the problem of realistic career planning, Kay presents a problem of emotional immaturity and social maladjustment. Vocational counseling cannot be isolated from her more fundamental needs. The careful counselor carries on vocational counseling, not only for its own results, but also as an experience for the counselee in self-appraisal and in developing habits of objectively viewing his own problems. The counseling process itself is intended to be a maturing experience and not just a decision-making activity.

Kay's low rating on the Verbal test indicates she will probably encounter difficulty in any reasonably good college if, indeed, she can manage to meet the entrance requirements. Were she emotionally stable and had she demonstrated her maturity in interpersonal relations, we might even agree that preparation for elementary school teaching would be a reasonable plan. If she could demonstrate genuine liking for chil-

Lola Bass

Problem: Lola needed reassurance about her program and some resolution of the conflict with her father about entering college.

Tests

Differential Aptitude Tests. Grade 10.
Otis Q-S, Beta. Grade not stated. IQ-127.
Cleeton Interest Inventory. Grade 10. Highest interest—secretarial.

Report of Counseling in Grade 10

Lola came to the counselor to talk about preparing for college. She is earning straight A's in the secretarial course. There is evidence of some family conflict on the issue of her immediate plans; her father objects to her going to college. Lola decided to stay in the secretarial course.

Comments

If Lola continues in her program she probably will be earning within a few years as much as many girls with college degrees. She looks like

Kay Bacall (concluded)

dren and evidence of competence in handling them and, in addition, if she were personally well adjusted, we could think of these as assets compensating her only average intelligence. But with two strikes against her—scholastic and personal—she probably is not a good candidate for a teachers college.

It is hoped that the counselor can probe a bit deeper into Kay's emotional tensions and help her mature at an accelerated pace before the end of Grade 12. Then she might be able to attain one or another of her goals.

This case constitutes a clear challenge to that decreasing minority of guidance personnel who still believe that competence in curricular and vocational counseling need not be founded on psychological training and clinical competence. Kay demonstrates that a sound background in developmental psychology and psychodynamics is a requisite for the modern counselor.

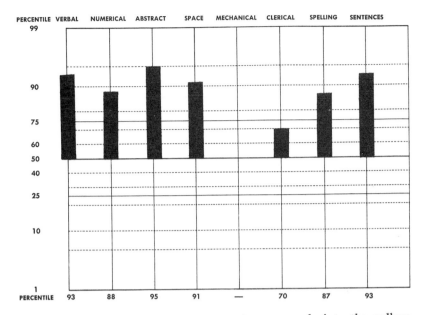

PERCENTILE	VERBAL	NUMERICAL	ABSTRACT	SPACE	MECHANICAL	CLERICAL	SPELLING	SENTENCES
PERCENTILE	93	88	95	91	—	70	87	93

the kind of girl any counselor is tempted to persuade into the college preparatory course; in fact, it is his obligation to be certain that such bright pupils are aware of their abilities, their opportunities, and the associated requirements.

But it does not necessarily follow that *all* bright girls should go to college. Other factors—such as financial resources, family aspirations and personal goals—are also involved. In this case, the counselor has done his primary duty by informing Lola about her abilities and the types of career to which she might aspire. One does wonder, however, whether she might not carry a modified course, combining her steno-graphic subjects with the minimum requirements for college entrance so that she can have freedom of decision should a college education seem more feasible to her and her parents later on. Assuming she has appropriate personal qualities, Lola can expect a high degree of suc-cess as a secretary. As a matter of fact, a secretarial course enriched with good general academic courses should produce not only a capital secretary but a useful citizen and interesting person as well—with or without college. The counselor's role is to make sure that both Lola and her father realize the facts about Lola's opportunities for further ed-ucation and employment, and that they consider these facts in their decisions. The factual approach with the profile can be helpful in the "education" of the father.

Katherine North

Problem: Katherine, without plans and clear ambitions, must outline her next educational steps.

Tests

Differential Aptitude Tests. Grade 10.
Stanford-Binet. Kindergarten. IQ-115.
Otis S-A, Higher. Grade 10. IQ-108.
Various reading tests in Grades 1 to 5; scores usually showed her one grade level or more advanced.
Stanford Achievement. Grade 8 (8.2). Grade equivalents: Reading—10.1, Language Usage—10.0, Arithmetic—7.2, Literature—7.6, Social Studies—8.0, Science—12.9, Spelling—6.2.
Cooperative Reading. Grade 10. 82d percentile.

Report of Counseling in Grades 10 and 11

Katherine's entire elementary school record presents a picture of a happy, well-adjusted, exceptionally well-cared-for child whose achievements were slightly better than one would expect from her ability. This probably was due to exceptional educational advantages in the home—trips, books, friends, etc.—and to the "halo" effect on teachers' grades of an attractive, bright-looking, well-mannered child.

In junior high school her grades, in comparison with those of her classmates, were not high. In Grade 10 she began to have some difficulty in maintaining the better-than-average academic record to which her parents were accustomed. Eleventh grade counseling dealt with vocational choices. She was having some difficulty with foreign language and, as a result, experienced a sense of frustration and defeat.

Looking for special aptitudes, interests or abilities, the counselor found in the *Differential Aptitude Tests* a profile with no outstanding high spots or low spots, except the inferior score on Spelling; similar weakness had also appeared two and four years earlier in the *Stanford Achievement Test.* In the interview, Katherine seemed, again, a pleasantly ordinary girl so far as personality was concerned; alert and anxious to be agreeable, but with no particular interests except artificial ones growing out of music lessons, well-managed social contacts, etc.

Having been taught by her family to expect to excel, and now faced with the necessity for increasingly serious academic effort and the development of special interests, Katherine finds herself at a loss. Her parents, too, are puzzled because Katherine seems not to have developed the initiative, self-reliance and independence normally attained at the

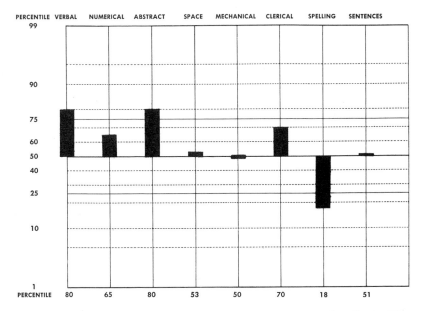

PERCENTILE	VERBAL	NUMERICAL	ABSTRACT	SPACE	MECHANICAL	CLERICAL	SPELLING	SENTENCES
PERCENTILE	80	65	80	53	50	70	18	51

junior year of high school by a student looking toward college. Her achievement test scores, school grades (a straight C average except for a couple of D's in foreign language), and *Differential Aptitude Test* scores give no evidence of outstanding ability or of outstanding interest in any one area.

At the time this report was written, she had not been given the *Kuder Preference Record* (part of this school's usual Grade 11 testing program). Quite possibly it could offer some help. Katherine may go through a difficult period in which she ceases to lean on her parents for direction and casts about to find interests of her own. She will need some exploratory courses and a good deal of counseling to help her interpret her experiences. This process may not crystallize into a clear-cut vocational and educational plan which is her own and which is within the limits of her capacity until after she has been out of high school a year or two. Junior college is being suggested as a sensible next step.

Comments

This case illustrates the moderately able girl who seems to have no goals. No doubt she can go to some college if her parents insist and if she wishes to follow the same stereotyped, planned life she has experienced thus far. Her uneven language skills (low in spelling, average in grammar, and superior in reading) suggest need for remedial work in Grades 11 and 12 if she wishes to cope with the demands of college or any post-high-school education of which her parents would approve;

53

e.g., a secretarial course. In fact, if her language skills are improved she probably could earn reputable grades in a not-too-demanding college—provided, further, that she develops some crystallized interests and attitudes of self-determination.

The *Differential Aptitude Tests,* in this case, predict mediocrity of performance in the kind of educational competition the parents envisage. However, the counselor can probably use the test profile also to show her (a) that she has more ability than her grades seem to show and, (b) that she needs to improve her language skills. Counseling along these lines and helping her develop some vital purposes will be tasks for the counselor in the next three semesters.

The counselor noted an eagerness to be agreeable on Katherine's part. This sort of observation is apt to be worth more than any number of scores on personality tests. Occasionally, such an urge to ingratiate oneself may be symptomatic of deep-seated insecurity, and referral to a clinical psychologist or psychiatrist may be indicated. Practically, however, it is usually the counselor's aim to help mobilize such traits as assets. A wish to please others is one of the most important keys to success in many jobs: receptionist, complaint clerk, tour guide, information counter attendant, and so on. (And, in the case of Katherine, it may be noted that many of these positions make no particular demand on ability to spell!)

A good counselor should never forget that most of the girls he counsels will one day be married. Important though their immediate vocational and educational decisions may be, they will spend more years as wives and mothers than in school or in any job. This may be considered only in passing or not at all in the counseling of girls who have clear-cut vocational aptitudes or interests for the next few years of their lives. But sometimes—and particularly when a girl is without strong tendencies toward any other occupation—it may be most constructive to focus her plans consciously on becoming in time a housekeeper and a mother. This means taking into account, in the choice of the next school or job, two extra points: the extent to which the experience will be useful later in making a home, and the frequency with which it will bring her into contact with congenial young men.

Gene Pratt

Problem: Gene was concerned about his grades, which were not as high as his family expected them to be.

Tests

Differential Aptitude Tests. Grade 9.

Otis Classification. Grade 8. Percentile rank—64.

Stanford Achievement. Grade 6 (6.8). Grade equivalents: Reading—6.8, Language—6.3, Spelling—6.8, Arithmetic—6.0.

Cooperative Reading. Grade 9. Percentile ranks: Vocabulary—33, Speed—62, Level—36.

Cooperative Biology. Grade 9. Percentile rank—38.

Kuder Preference Record. Grade 9. Details not given; report said all scores were below average.

Report of Counseling in Grades 9 and 10

Gene came for counseling late in his ninth-grade year to find an answer to his father's question as to why a boy who worked so faithfully did not receive higher grades. He is now in the tenth grade. The counselor had talked to Gene several times during the past year. Through the eighth and ninth grades, his problems were the rather routine ones of a growing boy. However, at the end of the first semester of the tenth grade, he received an F in Geometry. His father was hard on him because it was Gene's first failure. The boy was disturbed when he sought advice and reassurance.

Gene's father and mother were born in Germany and came to America as young people. They still speak German most of the time at home. His father holds a regular job during the day and sells insurance evenings and in his spare time; he is a dominating, firm, yet kindly gentleman who evidently provides much motivation for Gene's thought and behavior. Gene is the only child, is very well mannered, with an engaging smile and a fine, healthy appearance.

The father has decided that his son must finish a high school course of study which will permit his entrance into college prior to training in the field of insurance. He has selected the specific college. Evidently, no consideration has been given to any of the problems at hand. Gene's academic grades (D's and a few C's) agree with the pattern of test results shown on the profile. Yet his father insists he must take algebra, geometry and a language because the college he selected requires them.

It is the counselor's belief that a pleasing smile, fine attitude, and

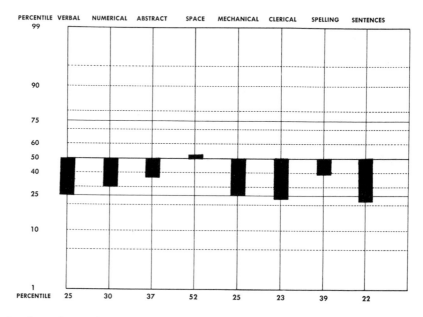

PERCENTILE	VERBAL	NUMERICAL	ABSTRACT	SPACE	MECHANICAL	CLERICAL	SPELLING	SENTENCES
PERCENTILE	25	30	37	52	25	23	39	22

hard work are keeping this boy going. Thus far counseling has been with Gene alone, who has not been able to cope with his father's insistence. Conferences including both the father and the son will no doubt be necessary if a satisfactory solution is to be found.

Comments

Good discipline and excellent work habits should probably be rewarded in themselves. Unfortunately his father has long-time plans for Gene which may be unattainable. That he can learn some vocation well and bring to it disciplined work habits seems evident—but his success probably will not be via the college route. The present report is brief. It has merely posed the problem. As the counselor states, the next steps —during the rest of Grade 11 and during Grade 12—ought, if possible, to include the father.

Experienced counselors can contribute to counseling practices by reporting in the professional literature some of their successful and less successful experiences in the "letting down" process. This delicate operation requires an understanding of the ego-involvement of parents in the careers of their children—parents working out their frustrations through their children, the social class consciousness of families, and the normal struggle for a better life. Decisions will frequently be made by force of the academic standards of schools and colleges or of the hiring standards of employers. The school counselor bears a responsibility, however, for trying to anticipate such painful collisions with reality and for be-

56

ing as helpful as possible in cases where he can assist only in picking up the pieces.

The counselor usually is more familiar with the principles of mental hygiene than most of the advisors the student meets, in school or out. He can try to forestall some of the problems by discovering those boys and girls with unrealistic plans as early as possible, so that changes in family thinking can take place over a period of time in a deliberate, less tense atmosphere.

Let us assume for a moment that Gene and his family have agreed to a modification of the family ambitions. What then can a counselor say regarding a plan for Gene? His profile is essentially a flat one. There is nothing distinguished about it. It is considerably below average.

There is no reason to assume because of his test scores and indifferent school success that Gene cannot succeed as an insurance salesman or in a clerical capacity in an insurance agency. It may be that the father can be persuaded to relinquish the academic goal when the vocational aspiration is not contradicted.

It is at this point that serious consideration should be given to the excellent work habits Gene possesses. The conferences with him and his family should lead to an exploration of his expressed and measured interests. However, his interests as recorded on the *Kuder Preference Record* are also uncrystallized and at a relatively low level. Perhaps in the rearranging of the school program it may possible for the counselor to arrange some exploratory experiences in the form of part-time, after school, or vacation jobs. These experiences should be such as will be genuinely accepted by Gene. And, of course, the counselor or other school representative who is in charge of such vocational exploratory programs should follow up with periodic conferences.

With his apparently fine work habits and general attitudes, Gene's vocational future will depend primarily on his developing an interest in some occupational field at a level which is appropriate to his abilities. In the meantime we should not forget that, not only his vocational planning, but also his general education is important to Gene, especially because of the value that the family seems to place on education.

Allen Smith

Problem: Allen is failing in school and is frequently truant.

Tests

> *Differential Aptitude Tests.* Grade 10.
> *Otis Q-S, Beta.* Grade not reported. IQ-83.

Report of Counseling in Grade 10

Allen is retarded; in the tenth grade, he is 17 years of age. He is in a commercial course. He is failing but his parents insist he must stay in school. Truancy is his way of reacting to failure and to parental pressures. The *Differential Aptitude Test* profile shows a clear-cut lack of aptitude for commercial subjects; he scores practically at the bottom on the Verbal, Clerical, Language Usage, and Numerical Ability tests. The two relatively bright spots in his aptitude pattern are the percentiles of 43 and 50 in Space Relations and Mechanical Reasoning.

Allen was offered transfer to the machine shop course in the vocational school but he rejected this plan and decided to remain in the present program. He is still failing and is frequently truant.

Comments

The *Differential Aptitude Test* profile yielded data which are of vital importance in this case. Allen's assets, while not strong, are distinctly differentiated. What can a counselor do when a boy "refuses" to accept the opportunity to transfer? We can assume that more extended counseling or more effective counseling might have accomplished the desired goal. Perhaps the counselor had such a big load that he could not pursue the case further. Perhaps he saw a futile situation.

Without the *Differential Aptitude Test* scores and only the evidence of a low IQ, this case might have *seemed* simpler. Shunting dull-normal boys into the easiest courses available and tolerating their low achievement until they drop out of school seems such an easy solution—until one begins to ask, "Which easy courses?" The knowledge that Allen has relatively strong ratings on two of the tests makes failure in counseling more poignant since the responsibility was placed on the counselor to try to effect a shift of program in the light of the test results.

Cases like this are particularly challenging to the counselors who operate consistently on the philosophy that the counselee is fully responsible for his own decisions. Even though it is technically possible to move a student from one course to another by administrative decision, counselors today prefer to develop an understanding on the part

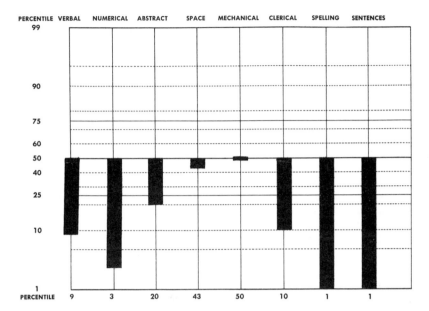

PERCENTILE	VERBAL	NUMERICAL	ABSTRACT	SPACE	MECHANICAL	CLERICAL	SPELLING	SENTENCES
PERCENTILE	9	3	20	43	50	10	1	1

of the counselee of what the problem is and what solutions are possible. They endeavor to help the counselee move from understanding to emotional acceptance of a better plan of action. This means that they must try to go beyond the overt behavior and seek an understanding of the reasons for the apparent obstinacy of the counselee in the face of facts.

As noted above, this understanding of the situation and acceptance of its implications was a matter not only for Allen but also for his parents. Considerable probing may be necessary to determine the reasons for resistance and, in the presence of heavy case loads and many other responsibilities, the counselor may have to just skip the case and move on to another which is more hopeful. We do not know the details of Allen's conflict with his family nor why he was so adamant about not changing his course of study. The following factors might show up in a more intensive study: anxieties regarding any kind of change; feelings of status with regard to the particular school (in a city with four special high schools), course of study, or subjects; personal loyalties built around the class in school or smaller social groups attending that school; vague feelings that a change in the curriculum is obvious evidence of failure which one cannot tolerate. The reader can think of many other possibilities but these are among the reasons why changing a person's life pattern is not merely a matter of laying out the data on the table and saying, "See here, this is a good plan of action."

At the time of reporting, the counselor still had a task cut out for him — but it probably will disappear unhappily, since the best guess is that Allen will soon drop out of school.

59

Charles White

Problem: Charles, in the face of failure, needed to consider a curricular change; the college preparatory course was not appropriate for his abilities.

Tests

Differential Aptitude Tests. Grade 10.
Otis S-A, Higher. Grade 10. IQ-104.
ACE Psychological Examination, High School. Grade 11. Percentile ranks: L-50, Q-50, Total—49.
Cooperative Reading. Grade 9. 30th percentile. Also Grade 10. 35th percentile.

Report of Counseling in Grades 10 and 11

Charles entered the college preparatory program in senior high school. During the first semester he experienced great difficulty in his studies of English, world history and Latin. Conferences with Charles and his mother revealed that the family was determined that Charles should have a college education. Charles wished to oblige his family and was working very diligently toward this goal. By the end of this semester, however, his failure in Latin and his low grades in English and history seemed to climax the discouragement under which he had been laboring through the past few years in school.

When he entered senior high, reading tests, junior high school achievement tests and intelligence tests had cast doubt on the advisability of his pursuing an academic program. At that time, the *Differential Aptitude Test* results also became available. They seemed to confirm the previous indications of Charles' limited verbal ability. At the same time they pointed out areas of superior ability, a positive starting point from which to plan revisions in Charles' high school program.

In the light of this new information, it was decided that Charles might further explore his interests in mechanical and technical work. He was assigned to less demanding class sections in English and history. Latin was replaced by mechanical drawing. At the end of the year, his marks and his disposition had improved considerably. In Grade 11 he is pursuing a high school program made up chiefly of shop, science and mathematics courses, and his work is entirely satisfactory. His present goal, in which his family now concurs, is to enter a technical training institute in a two-year college. There is good reason to believe he can complete such a course successfully.

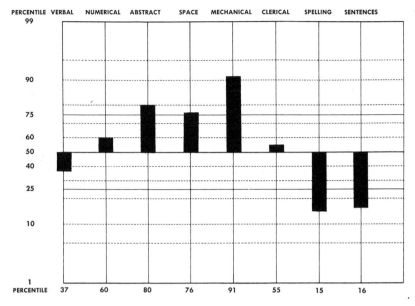

(It is interesting to note, but hard to explain, that the *ACE Psychological Examination* failed to differentiate between this boy's linguistic and quantitative abilities, whereas there seems to be a sharp difference shown in the *Differential Aptitude Test* scores.)

Comments

The counselor's report is quite complete. This boy apparently has talents in the areas of Abstract Reasoning, Space Relations and Mechanical Reasoning which would not be disclosed by verbally loaded tests or the standard curriculum.

Perhaps the junior high school counselors should have been alert to the pressure for achievement under which Charles was functioning willingly and doggedly. In this particular school system the junior and senior high school guidance programs are quite separate; there is, by and large, no systematic plan for checking up on unexceptional boys until they call attention to themselves by such means as failing their college preparatory courses in Grade 10.

In too many schools only the unusually dull pupils or the obviously maladjusted ones who create crises in their junior high classes force the issue of the need for curricular changes quite early. There seems to be a large neglected group — the average youngsters, who get along in the run-of-the-mill work of junior high and who seem to have clear plans. "Of course, Charles is to take the college preparatory course." Difficulties in language study and higher mathematics are often the first signals that these children, though perhaps wonderfully loyal and hard-working, are below average in the abilities required for a college preparatory program.

This situation argues for surveying aptitudes and achievements thoroughly in the second semester of Grade 8 or the first semester of Grade 9. It also argues for adequate staff time to permit careful analysis of the aptitudes and achievement (both from the cumulative record and the current testing) of each child. Special observation should be made of those pupils in whose records discrepancies appear. This should include (or be followed by) conferences with the parents. Sometimes administrative actions regarding the pupil's program or plans for a program are indicated.

This is not to say that under such a counseling plan Charles should be prohibited from trying algebra and Latin in Grade 9. If earlier counseling had occurred, the "repair counseling" in Grades 10 and 11 might have been less necessary and less painful for the parents since, we can assume, they themselves might have accepted suggestions about a change a year earlier.

Finally, here again we have a boy whose verbal abilities argue against his preparing for a liberal arts course but whose special abilities suggest an appropriate plan of further education in high school, and even beyond that, for a useful career.

Grade 9
Cases

Peter Ellis

Problem: Peter, a boy of little ability, had planned to prepare himself for entering engineering school.

Tests

Differential Aptitude Tests. Grade 9.

Report of Counseling in Grade 9

Peter transferred to this high school from a small school in a neighboring town. His previous school record was fair—he had not failed any subjects, but most of his marks were C. There were no test results available for Peter and he could not remember having taken any tests.

In his first interview, Peter said that he wished to become an engineer. He had elected the college preparatory course in his first semester, taking algebra, English, French, and mechanical drawing. Peter seemed to lack social maturity and displayed few outside interests.

At the end of six weeks, he was failing in three subjects—algebra, English and French. His reading level was low. On the advice of his teacher, he was allowed to drop French and concentrate on his other subjects.

On the *Differential Aptitude Tests,* Peter's Numerical Ability score strongly suggested that he might have a great deal of difficulty with the advanced mathematics which would be necessary for his work in a technical school. His low scores on the Verbal, Abstract and Mechanical tests and mediocre performance on the Space test were also discussed with him; it was pointed out that these scores indicated that study in an engineering school would be extremely difficult, if not actually impossible, for him. The counselor discussed with Peter his low reading level (which had been reported by teachers) and his very poor work in spelling. It was explained that he would face college work under great handicaps and would have to work harder and longer than many of the others who would be in his classes. While all of this was done in an attempt to discourage the boy's interest in engineering, care was taken to prevent his feeling inferior because of the situation. The counselor knew that college work would be impossible for Peter but felt that he must arrive at this decision on his own.

Peter had been advised to investigate other fields of work and has had various semi-skilled and skilled trades suggested as possibilities. He has also been advised to consider changing his course of study next

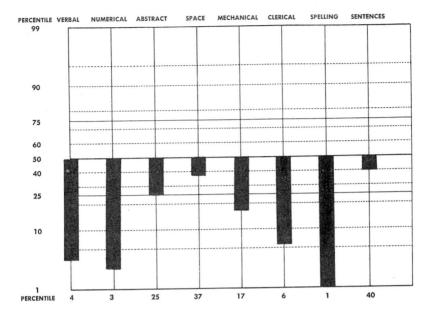

PERCENTILE	VERBAL	NUMERICAL	ABSTRACT	SPACE	MECHANICAL	CLERICAL	SPELLING	SENTENCES
PERCENTILE	4	3	25	37	17	6	1	40

semester to that required for entry into the commercial course in the tenth grade.

Comments

The reorientation of the excessively ambitious pupil is a delicate task requiring great skill and a willingness to wait until the pupil is ready to make his own discovery of what is best for him. At the same time, one cannot wait so long that a record of failures in too-difficult subjects has accumulated. The *Differential Aptitude Test* scores helped the counselor show Peter some of the specific difficulties he might have in an engineering program. Numerical Ability, Space Relations and Mechanical Reasoning have specific applicability in this counseling situation in a way that a single-score intelligence test or test of general scholastic ability would not.

Even if Peter chooses to change his program, another troublesome situation exists in the particular school system in which Peter is enrolled. Note that the counselor recommended his shifting to the commercial course. This is not a very good alternate for Peter; but *in Peter's school* it is almost the *only* other choice if there is no place for him in the college preparatory course. The sole advantage is that he probably will experience fewer failures in this somewhat easier course. Poor as they are for engineering, Peter's assets, nevertheless, are in the abilities measured by Abstract Reasoning and Space Relations. At best, some form of vocational program involving mechanical drawing and machine work

65

seems indicated. In discussions with us, this director of guidance has regretted that adequate opportunities along these lines are not available in his system.

The comments in the previous paragraph suggest that the *Differential Aptitude Tests* might be used for an analysis of the curricular needs of a community. The guidance director of this school system has done just that. He has analyzed the profiles of hundreds of ninth graders to determine, for example, how many boys are well below average on all tests except Space Relations and Mechanical Reasoning and are well above average on these two tests. He has found a considerable number of such boys. He has similarly analyzed the situation for girls. He has grouped other "types," such as those who are very low in everything but Verbal, Clerical and Language Usage and are only modestly high in these; his opinion is that these may be the girls who belong in the general commercial course. Although most testing is done for the purpose of solving the adjustment problems of pupils taken one at a time, aptitude testing programs also can be used to appraise the manner in which a school is adapting itself to the abilities characteristic of its students. There has been a long history of the use of achievement surveys to correct deficiencies in the curriculum. The newer trend of surveying pupils' aptitudes for the purpose of curricular planning is equally sensible.

William Swan

Problem: William was called in for counseling because his ambitions were too low in the light of his abilities.

Tests

Differential Aptitude Tests. Grade 9.
Otis Q-S, Beta. Grade 9. IQ-118.

Report of Counseling in Grade 9

The counselor became concerned because this boy, obviously of superior ability and with an excellent grammar school record, was enrolled in a four-year terminal agricultural course. From such a program William could continue with a two-year course at the state university but could not enter the regular course of work toward a degree.

On the basis of the *Differential Aptitude Test* scores, substantiated by the teachers' reports that William had become the first-ranking student in the agricultural department, the counselor invited the boy in for a conference. William's plans for the future, the *DAT* results, and his work in the agriculture course were discussed in detail. William expressed dissatisfaction with the agricultural program since he felt that he wanted "to learn more."

In a subsequent interview, the requirements for schools offering degree courses in agriculture were explored. After he had acquired this information, William felt that he would like to attend a college which grants degrees. However, he doubted that he would be able to secure the necessary funds.

At the counselor's request William's father came for an interview. College entrance requirements and costs as well as William's potentialities for success in college were discussed. The father showed understanding of these topics and made it clear that he would be able to provide sufficient funds for the boy's education. The counselor also discussed the possibility of scholarship assistance if William continued to earn superior grades.

On the basis of the assembled information and the boy's own determination, as well as that of his family, arrangements were made for William to transfer to the college preparatory course. In his first year in high school William has done honors work, receiving five grades of Excellent and three of Good.

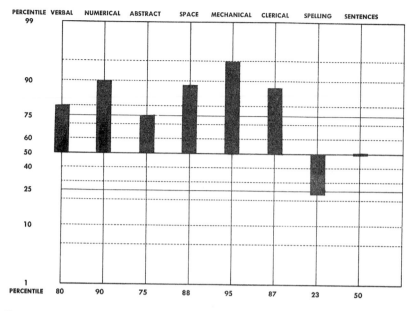

PERCENTILE	VERBAL	NUMERICAL	ABSTRACT	SPACE	MECHANICAL	CLERICAL	SPELLING	SENTENCES
PERCENTILE	80	90	75	88	95	87	23	50

Comments

This case illustrates the role of the counselor in identifying the superior child — and especially one who has made plans for an education and career which are less than appropriately ambitious. Technically, William was not a "problem." There was no crisis necessitating counseling; he was getting along fine. However, in keeping with an educational philosophy which holds that human talents are vital national assets, the counselor felt an obligation to stimulate William to explore better ways to work out his deep-seated interest in agriculture as a career.

A higher level of aspiration was both possible and acceptable to William and his parents. In other instances, the counselor may run into blocks of one kind or another — such as lack of ambition, financial difficulties, lack of curricular opportunities, etc.; but the counselor has a professional obligation to try to overcome these difficulties. The *Differential Aptitude Tests,* administered as a schoolwide survey program, represent an approach that is particularly valuable because it permits identification, not only of the generally superior youngster, but also of the pupil who has particularly strong assets along some lines and only moderate abilities in others.

This case also illustrates the need for a factual approach — through test data and through career information. Note that William was unaware of his full capabilities and furthermore thought that his family could not help him in college. The counselor brought father and son

68

together in a serious discussion of William's ambitions and abilities and how they could best be developed — probably the first discussion on this topic for which facts rather than feelings were available to them. Needless to add, this case represents one of the most pleasant and rewarding types of work for the counselor.

One guidance director suggests that whenever a whole class has been examined with the *Differential Aptitude Tests,* a sorting should be made of the profiles, identifying those students whose profiles show generally high ability and those with generally low ability. Then the counselors should systematically review these cases in terms of their present curricular status and past achievements. Where discrepancies in plans and abilities are observed, individual conferences should be arranged. Those with generally low abilities who are striving for inordinately high goals usually show up as counseling cases, chiefly because they experience failure and either come themselves or are sent. If they can be reached before the crisis, so much the better. The generally superior pupils who are taking too simple a program may never show up because they are breezing through school with ease; but quite a few appear in the counselor's office in their twelfth grade — too late for effective help — and raise searching questions in the counselor's mind about why they were not helped earlier to plan for careers commensurate with their abilities. It should not be necessary to add that this initial quick survey of the very low and very high students should be followed by a systematic review of all, including the "middles," who also may set their goals too high or too low.

The question might be raised as to why it is necessary to move William from a combination vocational-agricultural course and a general educational program into the formal college preparatory course. Why could he not stay in the program as originally planned and enter the college level agricultural program? The answer is that while some colleges and universities would consider his admission from the original program if he had a high achievement record and showed ability, maturity and purposefulness, most institutions would insist on a rather specific pattern of studies as a requirement for admission. The bright young boy who has ambitions to enter college should play safe by taking the proper preparatory program.

Cecelia Thomas

Problem: Cecelia has failed to adjust to school; her difficulties are aggravated by a poor home situation.

Tests

> *Differential Aptitude Tests.* Grade 8.
> *Stanford-Binet.* Grade 3. IQ-98.
> An *Otis* test. Grade 6. IQ-103.

Report of Counseling in Grade 9

Cecelia did good work in Grade 7. In Grade 8 her work and attitudes became very poor. A difficult family situation led to her being sent to live with an aunt in another state. In the fall she returned to this school to enter Grade 9 and showed great improvement for a while in appearance, attitudes and work habits. In a few weeks, however, she lapsed into her previous behavior. Counseling in the school is almost hopeless; she will not talk nor cooperate. Out-of-school factors seem most important in this case. She has been referred to a family service organization.

Comments

The use of the *Differential Aptitude Test* data for educational and vocational counseling with this girl is likely to be unprofitable until her general problems of adjustment are resolved or ameliorated. The school, not having a full clinical service, has wisely referred this case to an outside agency. Normally it would be expected that these data would be made available to the psychologist in the outside agency. The *Differential Aptitude Test* scores are not consistent with the earlier *Binet* and *Otis* ratings. Because none of her *DAT* ratings approaches the 50th percentile (as compared with earlier IQs of 98 and 103), we can suspect that she now is either unable or unwilling to show her abilities on a test. This situation illustrates the use of discrepant ability test ratings as clues to the presence of other debilitating problems. Cecelia should be retested when and if improvement has occurred in

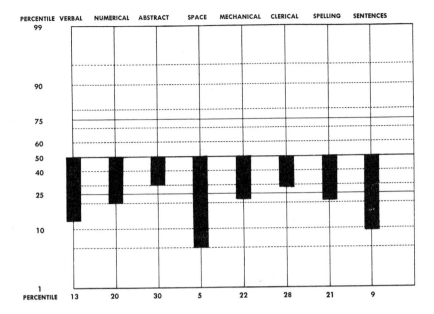

her environment and after she has responded to therapy. At present we are not certain what her abilities really are. Children scoring high *must* have known the right answers. Children scoring low, although usually of limited ability, *may* have performed poorly as a result of emotional disturbances. Whenever a low-scoring case also shows clinical symptoms, we need to defer judgment as to the child's true level of abilities.

Constance Turse

Problem: Constance, with no real problem, sought advice about her educational plans.

Tests

Differential Aptitude Tests. Grade 9.
Otis Q-S, Beta. Grade 7. IQ-129.
Iowa Silent Reading. Grade 7. Reading age equivalent—18.

Report of Counseling in Grade 9

Constance has a distinctive speaking voice. She expresses herself clearly and in good English. Her health record is good; she has no outstanding defects. Her varied interests include playing the piano, reading, and playing softball. Constance began to take piano lessons when she was in the sixth grade; she has become steadily more interested in music. Last year she decided to specialize in classical rather than popular music. Her grades last year were excellent in every subject.

Constance has no vocational preference. She says she wants to go to college but doesn't know which one.

In this case the *Differential Aptitude Tests* are consistent with other information. As the *Manual* states, superior students often score low on the Clerical Speed and Accuracy test. This proved true in the case of Constance. After the counselor had stressed to Constance the importance of speed, she was retested. Her second score for this test placed her in the 76th percentile for girls on local norms. (Some of this gain, of course, may have been due to practice.)

Comments

In a school which tests all its students in the eighth or ninth grade, the early discovery (or, as in this case, verification) of talent becomes administratively simple. Constance really has no problem requiring intensive counseling now. The counselor, however, is distinctly aware of her as a high-level achiever from whom society can expect much, and therefore a pupil who needs the very best training commensurate with her abilities. Care should be taken to prevent her coasting through

72

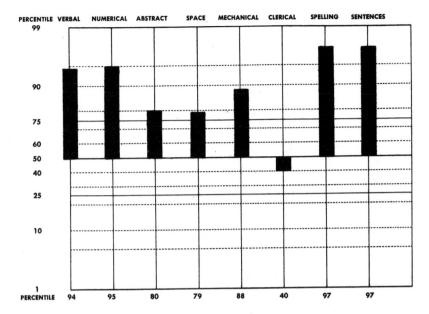

high school with deteriorating work habits or finding herself frustrated by lack of direction.

We shall assume that the counselor has, or can develop, a plan for effective communication to the teachers about girls like Constance. Constance needs exposure to information about — or better yet, bits of experience in — the more challenging occupations open to able women.

James Wallace

Problem: James' ambitions seem too high in the light of tested abilities and his previous record.

Tests

Differential Aptitude Tests. Grade 9.
Two recent *Otis* tests. Grades not reported. IQs-103; 104.

Report of Counseling in Grade 9

James is a tall, good-looking boy with an air of self-confidence. He speaks well in class and makes a very good first impression which is not always followed up by satisfactory marks in written work.

He is ambitious and is financially able to go to college. His chief aim has been to prepare for law and a secondary aim has been to become a teacher. On the basis of some success in English work he also has expressed ambitions to become a journalist.

James' parents came to school to discuss his vocational and educational aims. A discussion of the results of the *Differential Aptitude Tests* and his scholastic record made it clear to them that his intent to enter law was too ambitious. They felt that his abilities would, however, be sufficient for him to study for the teaching profession.

After reading occupational information, James agreed that the study of law would be beyond him. He felt that he would like teaching, but would want to be a college professor. He is gradually scaling down this aim as he gets into the study of algebra and languages and is now beginning to accept the idea of going to a teachers college and preparing for elementary school teaching.

Comments

One wonders why the discrepancy between the *Otis* ratings (slightly above average) and the *DAT* picture (all below average) was not probed. Perhaps an individual examination should have been made, or some of the *DAT* tests (Verbal, Numerical and Abstract, for instance) verified by giving Form B to him individually so as to assure better rapport. The counselor may have had other information on which to reject this suggestion. Unless both school grades and the *DAT* profile are concealing an emotional problem, the counseling in this case seems to have been in the proper direction; although one is constrained to doubt his ability to succeed in a teachers college.

The counselor used the *Differential Aptitude Test* information and

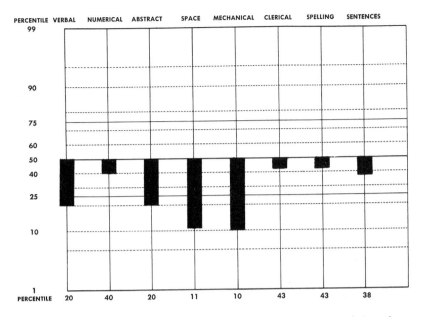

PERCENTILE	VERBAL	NUMERICAL	ABSTRACT	SPACE	MECHANICAL	CLERICAL	SPELLING	SENTENCES
1 PERCENTILE	20	40	20	11	10	43	43	38

James' previous achievement record to set the stage for a careful evaluation of educational and vocational plans by James and his family. A study of the requirements for a career in law also helped James to reach his own conclusions. Even his current goal of preparing for teaching probably is ambitious, but for the time being the counselor presumedly is wise in not disturbing the boy's ego further. It appears that the scaling-down process is continuing. As a matter of fact, James possibly can gain admission to some less-demanding teacher-training school if he makes a reasonable record in high school. Personal qualities other than abilities will also have to be considered in relation to teaching.

The counselor has the obligation to follow this boy carefully because James' motivation to do well in school may deteriorate if his family's expectancies and his real achievements are too far out of line with each other. The *DAT* profile is fairly flat. The counselor has little basis in the tests for suggesting any special vocational training, except that the relatively low Space Relations and Mechanical Reasoning scores argue against technical education. He may have potentialities as a satisfactory clerical worker, perhaps a successful bank teller or hotel clerk; his assurance and appearance suggest selling as a career. Should such leads appear in his hobbies or other activities, they might suggest modifications in James' plans for the last year or two of high school.

75

Grade 8
Cases

Anne Jefferson

Problem: Anne sought help in connection with her educational plans; lacking in self-confidence, she had made some unduly hasty decisions about her career.

Tests

> *Differential Aptitude Tests.* Grade 8.
> *Otis Q-S, Beta.* Grade 7. IQ-100.
> *Stanford Achievement.* Grade 8. Grade equivalents: Paragraph Meaning — 10.8, Word Meaning — 9.9, Language Usage — 9.9, Spelling — 7.3, Arithmetic Computation — 9.6, Arithmetic Reasoning — 7.9, Social Studies — 6.8, Literature — 6.8, Science — 9.3.

Report of Counseling in Grade 8

The members of Anne's class had an opportunity to see their *Differential Aptitude Test* profiles before the personal counseling sessions. Anne was invited to discuss her *Differential Aptitude Test* profile in more detail. She said the *DAT* scores had been of no use to her but the counselor discovered in the interview that Anne had changed her elective choices for the ninth grade from general business to science on the basis of the tests, particularly the low Clerical rating. Since all her scores except those on the Clerical and Sentences tests were well above average, she was advised that she could carry a commercial course if that was what she really wanted. (This was considered correct, even though these two tests are highly relevant to commercial work.) The main purpose of this interview was to help Anne, who was having difficulties in making social adjustments, gain self-confidence in making decisions and acquire the habit of getting her facts straight before making those decisions. The effect was to establish the idea that the counselor was interested in her and could help her from time to time.

Comments

We must assume that the counselor was correct in noting that the girl's real interest lay in the commercial course rather than the science course in the ninth grade. No mention is made of discussion of college planning. She is a fairly able girl and probably could succeed in a not-too-demanding college. The counselor stated his first purpose in the eighth grade counseling as being the use of test data to help the pupil think more openly and confidently about herself. Perhaps the real planning for a career would best come toward the end of the ninth grade —

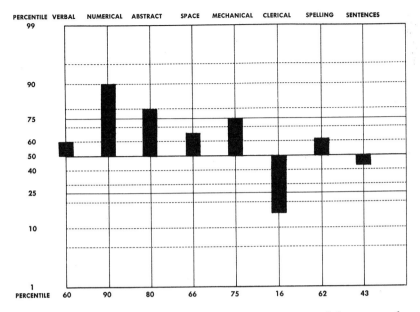

PERCENTILE	VERBAL	NUMERICAL	ABSTRACT	SPACE	MECHANICAL	CLERICAL	SPELLING	SENTENCES
PERCENTILE	60	90	80	66	75	16	62	43

or even later. If she does elect the complete commercial course, she should do well in it; but in our opinion other possibilities, involving college, should at least be considered during her ninth-grade year.

Note that Anne's *Otis* IQ of 100 is suspect on the basis of excellent rankings on the first five tests in the above profile; her Verbal Reasoning score is a little above average and is not too divergent from the *Otis* results. This demonstrates the inadequacies of single-score intelligence tests which are loaded heavily with verbal content. Also, on the Clerical test, and to a lesser extent on the *Otis,* she may have been handicapped by a too-cautious approach to speed tests.

As a final comment we question the practice of turning over test results to the pupils prior to counseling. We are informed that in this school the test results are presented on a group basis, and that sooner or later that year every pupil is counseled. Presumably this is considered a necessary time-saving procedure. We wonder whether it would suffice to present only a general discussion of the test program and its meaning. We feel that test results should not be given to pupils — certainly not to young ones — outside of the counseling interview. We know there is a difference of opinion on this matter and that some test authors actually promote the use of "self-interpreting" profiles. It is our firm belief that even the wisest counselors have considerable difficulty in interpreting test data in relation to all of the internal and external forces which govern educational, vocational and other personal decisions. Ninth-graders, or even college freshmen, cannot be expected to have the knowledge or skill to interpret test results without counseling aid.

John Ling

Problem: John was a scholastically retarded boy with a difficult home situation; in Grade 7 at age 15, special plans were necessary.

Tests

Differential Aptitude Tests. Grade 7.

Minnesota Rate of Manipulation. Grade 7. Percentile ranks: Turning — 90, Two-hand Turning and Placing — 60.

Report of Counseling in Grade 7 (special)

John, a rejected boy from a broken home, had been assigned to a state agency for foster home placement because he was not accepted by his stepfather. He had become greatly retarded and now, on entering this school at age 15, he was technically in Grade 7. Tentatively placed in an academic program pending examination for possible assignment to a special program, John did very well. His previous failures evidently were not due to lack of ability.

A special course in auto mechanics was planned with him. A year later John was doing B work in the shop and A and B work in the related courses. His attendance record was perfect. In his fourth semester in this school he was classed in Grade 11 and had near honor grades. He was working part time for an auto dealer.

Comments

A school has an obligation to examine carefully the causes of retardation. This report does not include any reference to appraisals by the state agency which had managed John. One wonders if he had been labeled dull over the years.

Fortunately the counselor took a constructive view: John is too old to be in Grade 7. What shall we do with him? What abilities does he have? On Grade 8 norms, appropriate for his grade level, he looked quite superior. His percentile ranks on Grade 10 norms (which are appropriate for a 15-year-old boy) are also plotted.

The counselor apparently felt it unwise to consider a regular aca-

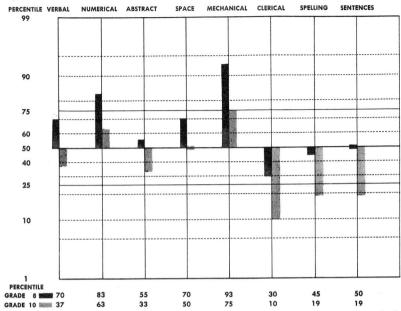

PERCENTILE	VERBAL	NUMERICAL	ABSTRACT	SPACE	MECHANICAL	CLERICAL	SPELLING	SENTENCES
GRADE 8	70	83	55	70	93	30	45	50
GRADE 10	37	63	33	50	75	10	19	19

demic program. While he reported only Grade 8 norms to us, it is likely that he discounted them and informally compared John with pupils his own age. He did not refer to John's interests, but these, even though not tested, may have influenced the counselor's recommendation.

As his deficiency in formal education is made up, his language skills may improve — unfortunately we do not have more recent grades or test scores. Despite educational handicaps John seems quite able, and the pattern suggests that the vocational plan which John will pursue is a sound one.

Harry Marks

Problem: Harry's mother has vocational ambitions for her son which seem to be inconsistent with his grades and test scores.

Tests

> *Differential Aptitude Tests.* Grade 8.
> *Stanford-Binet.* Grade 3. IQ-75. Also, Grade 4. IQ-86.
> An *Otis* test. Grade 7. IQ-88.

Report of Counseling in Grades 8 and 9

Harry shows a long history of slow progress, having been below his appropriate grade all through school. He came to his counselor while in Grade 8, very unhappy about having to go to special Hebrew classes two afternoons a week. His parents were preparing him to enter a Hebrew high school with the possibility that he might be trained later as a rabbi. Harry did not like the plan and was sure he could not do the work. In the spring of his eighth grade, his school record and *Differential Aptitude Test* profile were discussed with the mother. On the basis of this conference she agreed that Harry ought at least to complete his ninth grade in the public junior high school. She apparently was partially convinced of the unsoundness of her own plan. She agreed that Harry should be headed, as he wished, into the general clerical course. This decision was consistent with his strongest points, Clerical and Spelling. Harry is progressing well in this program in the ninth grade; during the fall semester his mother expressed her conviction that the correct decision had been made for Harry.

Comments

Counselors with factual data have a better basis for dealing with unrealistically ambitious mothers than do those who can speak only from vague information. The negative information that Harry is not college caliber was very important, but the positive information that Harry's best chances were in the general clerical program was just as important. After all, Harry's mother was being asked to give up a long-felt ambition to have her son become a rabbi, or at least some sort of learned man. We have no exact record of how the counselor was able to help her give up this status-laden aspiration in favor of Harry's own interests and abilities. The sequence included the school record, the test data, a counseling conference initiated by the boy and participated in by his mother, a short-term decision which would not preclude later

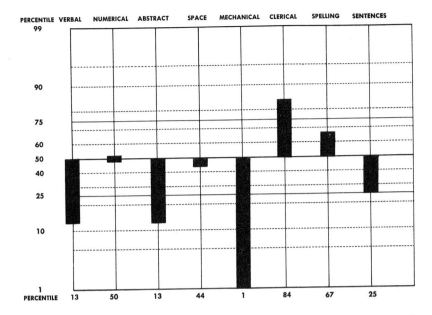

PERCENTILE	VERBAL	NUMERICAL	ABSTRACT	SPACE	MECHANICAL	CLERICAL	SPELLING	SENTENCES
PERCENTILE	13	50	13	44	1	84	67	25

reconsideration, actual tryout of a reasonable academic program, and a follow-up conference at which the mother, however reluctantly, was able to bring herself to express satisfaction with what had happened. Harry is on the way toward becoming a useful citizen trained for work which he can handle. Even though he is in a commercial course because this seems the best one for him, the chances are considerable that he will not achieve distinction as a clerical worker.

We still do not know whether there is any tendency for his family to reject him for having let his mother down; what evidence we have indicates that she has taken the changed role for Harry with good grace.

Gerald Oakton

Problem: Gerald, a boy who is generally poor in school work, was counseled as part of a regular Grade 8 program of educational and vocational planning.

Tests

Differential Aptitude Tests. Grade 8.
Otis Q-S, Beta. Grade 7. IQ-104.
Stanford Achievement. Grade 8. Grade equivalents: Paragraph Meaning — 9.0, Word Meaning — 7.7, Language Usage — 6.6, Spelling — 6.3, Arithmetic Computation — 6.5, Arithmetic Reasoning — 7.0, Social Studies — 8.8, Literature — 6.1, Science — 9.6.

Report of Counseling in Grade 8

Gerald had been very nervous and temperamental during his earlier school years. His achievement test scores more often are low than high. The high scores in Mechanical Reasoning and Space Relations, confirmed by his advanced achievement on the science test, helped him very much in deciding on his high school program. During the conferences Gerald set up a four-year sequence of courses with these abilities in mind; in Grade 9 he is doing well. The test results seemed to reinforce his confidence in himself — something that had been sadly lacking before.

(Late in Grade 9 the counselor added this information: Gerald had some difficulty this year . . . We do not have enough courses to meet his needs . . . Next year he can have more electives. He has been restless . . . He has not participated in many school activities.)

Comments

This is a profile which shows such extreme contrast between the peaks (Mechanical Reasoning and Space Relations) and the valleys (all the others) that counseling becomes fairly easy — if the school can provide Gerald with the courses in which he can capitalize on his strengths without too great demand on his lesser abilities. He obviously is not of college caliber. The exploratory trade program in the ninth grade leading to a more narrowed choice in later years was wise, even though the counselor later reported some difficulties because of the limitations of the curriculum in Grade 9. Since he is low in Numerical Ability he probably should be given some specialized arithmetic training to help him use his real talents better. Because his Verbal rating is

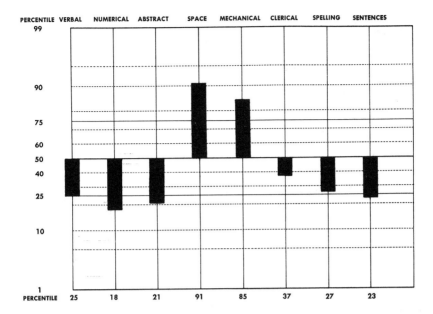

| PERCENTILE | 25 | 18 | 21 | 91 | 85 | 37 | 27 | 23 |

considerably poorer than his *Otis* rank, further checking of his abilities, say in Grade 10, is indicated; perhaps remedial work in the language skills will be worth while.

Gerald comes from a relatively small community and one which has not yet developed a full program of vocational education. Counselors in such situations are sometimes frustrated because of the limited educational opportunities for the counselee. However, a good counselor can offset such deficiencies if he is willing to consider the whole community as the educational workshop. It is usually possible to find stores, shops, small factories, and service organizations which will employ students on a part-time basis so as to provide opportunities for work experiences and vocational exploration. Many employers, of course, are not interested in such cooperative ventures at first. The time and effort required in organizing this kind of program should not be underestimated; but the rewards are great. If the counselor is willing to work slowly, and with a few interested employers at a time, he probably can develop a pattern of cooperation which is helpful, not only to the employer, but also to the boys and girls who go through the program.

Blanche Ridge

Problem: Blanche was seen as part of a regular program of educational planning in the eighth grade.

Tests

Differential Aptitude Tests. Grade 8.
Otis Q-S, Beta. Grade 7. IQ-96.
Stanford Achievement. Grade 8. Grade equivalents: Paragraph Meaning — 10.8, Word Meaning — 8.8, Language Usage — 7.9, Spelling — 6.5, Arithmetic Computation — 8.6, Arithmetic Reasoning — 9.9, Social Studies — 7.9, Literature — 7.0, Science — 9.9.

Report of Counseling in Grade 8

Blanche said she was helped by group discussion of the *Differential Aptitude Tests* and by studying her own test profile to learn that she needed to work very hard on spelling. She seemed to see little relationship between the tests and her plans for the future, but said she wanted to learn as much as she could about herself so she would make a wise vocational choice. Therefore, she was genuinely interested when she began to see that her scores might mean something in relation to specific occupations. She supposed she'd "just be a typist because of the low score in spelling which would mean I couldn't be a secretary." When asked if she really wanted this field, she said, hesitantly, "I'd really like dress designing but I couldn't do that, of course." It was explained that her *DAT* scores on Abstract Reasoning, Space Relations and Mechanical Reasoning were superior and that these aptitudes could have some bearing on success in dress designing and manufacturing. She left the counselor with a glow of enthusiasm that will surely lead to exploration, at least, of a field in which she may find a satisfying career.

Comments

Blanche's spelling status is surely out of line and suggests need for remedial training. The last line of the counselor's report carried the implication that, during the ninth grade, further testing and study of career requirements and opportunities would be helpful. Is her current

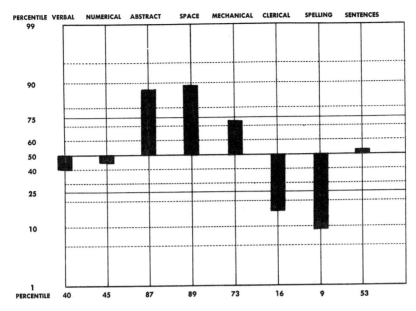

PERCENTILE	VERBAL	NUMERICAL	ABSTRACT	SPACE	MECHANICAL	CLERICAL	SPELLING	SENTENCES
PERCENTILE	40	45	87	89	73	16	9	53

interest in designing merely a "glamour response"? Should the interest in dress designing be directed toward the art aspects or the technical and production aspects? If this girl becomes interested in teaching, might training at the college level in home economics or practical arts be considered? It is hoped that the high school can provide Blanche with some tryout experiences to explore her expressed interest and observed aptitudes. Presumably she should be made aware at any rate that many more opportunities exist in teaching, dressmaking or in small dress shops than in designing for the big name lines.

Albert Roth

Problem: The school needed to diagnose the nature of the difficulty of a boy who had been considered of superior ability but who has had a persistent record of poor achievement.

Tests

Differential Aptitude Tests. Grade 8.

Stanford-Binet. Grade 1. IQ-125. Also, Grade 5. IQ-126. In Grade 9 this test was given again especially for this report: IQ-111.

Otis Q-S, Beta. Grade 7. IQ-92.

Stanford Achievement. Grade 9. Grade equivalents: Reading Ability — 6.6, Arithmetic — 6.6, Literature — 5.9, Spelling — 4.6.

Report of Counseling in Grades 8 and 9

In Grade 8, Albert did poor work in all school subjects, failing two subjects in June and barely passing the other two. The staff felt that Albert was very immature; in a conference with his teachers, the parents were strongly advised that he repeat Grade 8 completely. The results of the aptitude and achievement tests supported this decision. Albert's mother refused to accept the recommendation and blamed the school and the teachers' prejudices for his failures. She insisted that he be allowed to go to summer school and make up the failures. Against the advice of the counselor, he went to summer school and received the barely passing grade of 70 in the two subjects he had failed earlier. Under the circumstances, the school had to admit him to Grade 9. For the two grading periods of this term, he has failed in one subject and received just passing marks in the others.

His mother is working with him on spelling and arithmetic, but there is great doubt that he will be able to complete the ninth grade this year.

Additional Notes from Files of School Psychologist

Grade 1, January: Very inadequate to very superior on *Binet.* Most superior on tests dealing with language and vocabulary. Poor on practical tests. Overstimulated; taught "cute," precocious information at home on world situation and astronomy. School expected boy to test "near genius."

Grade 5, February: Retested because poor on all "tool" subjects, especially reading. Has been having remedial reading with Mrs. H and now with Mrs. N. Very poor reading attempt on *Binet* and *Gray Oral Reading Test.* Poor rote memory for digits and sentences. Wonderful fund of information. Helpful in any school situation. Beloved by teachers and pupils. Substituted for pupil absent from play; performed role better than original. Vision checked.

Grade 9, December: Poor scores on *Differential Aptitude Tests.* Failed some work last year. Passed some subjects in summer school. Poor work this year but better at last report. On group tests always tested below average. Reading has always been

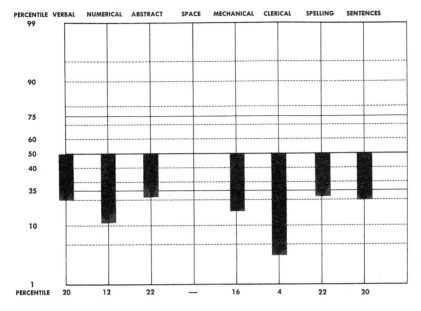

PERCENTILE	VERBAL	NUMERICAL	ABSTRACT	SPACE	MECHANICAL	CLERICAL	SPELLING	SENTENCES
PERCENTILE	20	12	22	—	16	4	22	20

inadequate for grade level. Remedial reading several years. Ambidextrous—may have affected reading, spelling and writing. Loves science, talks interestingly, but science paper spelled atrociously.

Talked with former principal who asserts that Albert was always one of the most resourceful, helpful, interesting students from Kindergarten through Grade 7. In early years stimulated by the home beyond his interests and age level. Always poor achievement. Conversed with mother regarding Reading Clinic. Mother quite disturbed about expense; referred for examinations by three vision specialists at various times. Mother tense when discussing husband's service in World War II; she feels his present work and income are not commensurate with his ability. Feels unable to afford Reading Clinic. Sister (in Grade 4) and Albert to get library science books to practice reading together. Mother also to help.

Comments

The staff of the school recognizes that it has not succeeded in narrowing the gap between Albert's presumed high intelligence and his obviously low achievement. Remedial reading attempts in earlier years seemed ineffective. The early reports of parental overdevotion and emphasis on precocious knowledge suggest that this boy may have developed considerable skill in nonacademic ways of satisfying his ego needs and of pleasing his teachers. Apparently he did not have to read and spell to seem effective and be well liked in school. This case points up the need for a psychological clinic in which the reading deficiency is studied and treated in a comprehensive setting, as a problem of both academic retardation and emotional health.

By now—Grade 9—Albert does not seem as bright as he once did. Whether his achievement level would rise after a year of extremely

Hans Soter

Problem: Hans' family, recent immigrants, were concerned about his adaptation to a new culture.

Tests

> *Differential Aptitude Tests.* Grade 8.
> *Stanford-Binet.* Grade 8. IQ-139.

Report of Counseling in Grade 8

A year before, Hans had entered the seventh grade in this school and done superior work. He had studied English in Germany for only

Albert Roth (concluded)

skillful reeducation in work habits and skill subjects is not certain. Note that he also ranks low on the nonverbal and less-scholastic tests—Abstract Reasoning, Mechanical Reasoning, and Clerical Speed and Accuracy—none of which should have been affected much by reading deficiency, although the latter is dependent on the perceptual abilities also needed in reading.

The school is considering the hypothesis that maybe this boy's personality may be deteriorating progressively as a consequence of the persistent unwise handling by his mother. The notes about the mother suggest that she may have helped develop a case for a mental hygiene clinic, and that simple remedial programs by classroom teachers will not suffice.

The role of the *Differential Aptitude Test* battery in this case is to challenge the older ratings which indicated that the boy was superior in intelligence. The recent *Binet* was given to check up on the discrepancy between the older *Binet* results and the new *Otis, Stanford Achievement* and *Differential Aptitude Test* records. The *DAT* profile calls attention to the current low scores in tests not primarily dependent on reading. The low *DAT* profile, and the consistently low achievement record, are clinical warnings which should prompt us to investigate further the causes of the great disparity between the early *Binet* and other ratings, as well as the smaller but still important discrepancy between the recent *Binet* IQ and current group test and achievement scores. It seems very likely that the earliest IQ reflected home coaching; on the other hand, the current *Binet* may be evidence of resources which (perhaps for emotional reasons) he cannot bring to bear on classroom work or paper-and-pencil group tests.

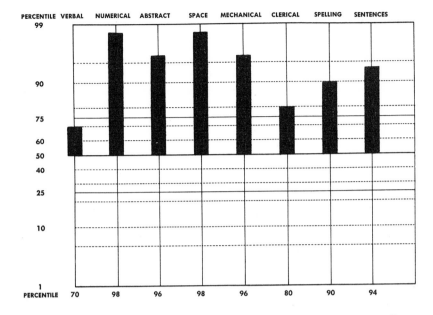

PERCENTILE	VERBAL	NUMERICAL	ABSTRACT	SPACE	MECHANICAL	CLERICAL	SPELLING	SENTENCES
PERCENTILE	70	98	96	98	96	80	90	94

one year, and his father naturally was concerned over his son's adjustment in the new world. The test data and his academic record clearly indicate that Hans is a very superior boy whose abilities have helped him overcome his language handicap.

Comments

This is obviously one of those pleasant counseling cases in which the main concern now is to help Hans arrange a suitable program for a high-level career. His weakest abilities, Verbal and Clerical, are more than adequate for most careers, and these most likely have been depressed by the language and cultural change. His outstanding ranks on the Numerical Ability, Abstract Reasoning, Space Relations, and Mechanical Reasoning tests offer good reason for encouraging him toward science or technology. However, his generally high standing on all eight tests indicates that insofar as these test data are concerned, he probably can achieve success in almost any career. It may be wisest to let his final decisions be determined by his interests and opportunities as they develop.

91

Susan Tenney

Problem: Susan, a girl about to enter ninth grade, was wondering about architecture as a possible career.

Tests

Differential Aptitude Tests. Grade 8.
Otis Q-S, Beta. Grade 7. IQ-114.
Stanford Achievement. Grade 8. Grade equivalents: Paragraph Meaning — 11.1, Word Meaning — 9.3, Language Usage — 7.7, Spelling — 6.3, Arithmetic Computation — 11.3, Arithmetic Reasoning — 9.6, Social Studies — 9.0, Literature — 11.3, Science — 9.9.

Report of Counseling in Grade 8

This girl said she had always wanted to be an architect. Her mother felt that she would not "meet the right people" in this field and would face unfair competition from men. She wanted her to study art. The girl, the mother and the counselor studied the *Differential Aptitude Test* profile together. The high scores in Numerical Reasoning, Abstract Reasoning, Space Relations, and Mechanical Reasoning helped the mother realize that the girl might be able to meet masculine competition in her chosen field. As a result, after some months of consideration, the mother has decided to let the girl make her own choice.

Comments

The above paragraph reads as if Susan had made a final choice. The reporting counselor, of course, realizes that plans may change again. The counselor's main aim so far seems to have been to help the mother understand the need for broader planning in the light of Susan's abilities and opportunities. While architecture is stressed now and the mother may have had some real basis for considering an art career appropriate, it is apparent that during the next few years Susan might well explore a whole family of careers. On one axis there is fine art itself and its variants—practical arts, recreational arts and crafts, commercial and advertising art, illustrating, occupational therapy, teaching of art in elementary and secondary schools, stage craft, etc. On the engineering side of the current architectural interest, she may later consider drafting and technical drawing. Careers in interior decorating, fashion, product or package designing, and the like might well be considered also.

The main thing now is that the test profile shows Susan's mental abilities to be such that her entry into any of several careers is possible.

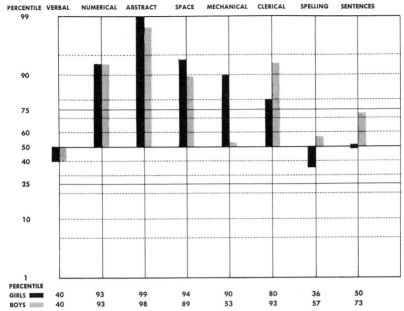

PERCENTILE	VERBAL	NUMERICAL	ABSTRACT	SPACE	MECHANICAL	CLERICAL	SPELLING	SENTENCES
PERCENTILE								
GIRLS	40	93	99	94	90	80	36	50
BOYS	40	93	98	89	53	93	57	73

The next steps are to evaluate her art ability by test and by actual tryout, and to have her study career information so she will know what the work in these fields is like and what is required in preparation. Clarification of the apparent discrepancy between her mediocre Verbal Reasoning score and her *Otis* and achievement test results might be sought in further testing.

We have also drawn Susan's profile showing how her scores compare with boys'—a comparison which is relevant if she expects to enter engineering or achitectural school and compete almost exclusively with boys. This sort of comparison is more meaningful at the eleventh or twelfth grade, but is made here because of Susan's interest in an architectural program. Note that she is average in Mechanical Reasoning on the boys' norms, which should constitute a warning since the average engineering student tends to be well above the median of all boys on this test.

As a matter of fact, this very serious attention to a specific career on Susan's part is not as important as the fact that she is concerned about taking her next educational steps wisely. She may end up with different plans by the time she is ready for college. In the meantime her program is necessarily a general one preparing her for college. Her concern about her own education is pleasantly in contrast with the indifference of those counselees with whom the main task is to locate some wisp of interest which can be developed into adequate motivation for staying in school.

Doris Watson

Problem: Doris hesitated to take algebra because she was afraid she might fail.

Tests

Differential Aptitude Tests. Grade 8.
An *Otis* test. Grade 6. IQ-99.

Report of Counseling in Grade 8

Doris was reported to be a conscientious but daydreaming worker, who did not follow directions until they had been repeated and then asked many questions about what to do. On the basis of her previous school record, Doris was advised to take algebra in the ninth grade, but she was not willing to tackle it for fear of failure. The counselor used the *Differential Aptitude Test* profile to help her understand that some of her abilities were superior and that she had little reason for thinking she might fail. She agreed to try, and now in the middle of the ninth year is carrying five major subjects with grades in the 80s.

Comments

This case illustrates the use of the scores on the eight *Differential Aptitude Tests* to aid a timid pupil both in setting goals that are reasonable and in overcoming unwarranted fears. Apparently this girl never before really knew how able she was; even superior children have qualms about their ability to cope with school subjects. Because Doris is relatively superior in a number of abilities, it is reasonable to suppose that she may be able to improve her performance somewhat in the Language Usage areas by individual tutelage or in remedial classes. The first step of the counselor was to get her into a curriculum which would challenge her; the next step would be to help her remove the spelling and grammar handicap.

Counseling Doris without the *DAT,* or similar tests, might well have resulted in letting her settle for less than reasonable goals. Her "intelligence" is greater than the IQ of 99 suggests. For verbal abilities the "average" label may be correct; for other abilities, the IQ of 99 is not a fair index. Fortunately, realistic goal-setting was helpful to her emotionally as well as career-wise.

This brief report of counseling is not intended to leave the reader with a feeling that a single dose of reassurance will usually help a counselee reorganize his concepts of himself. Competent counselors do

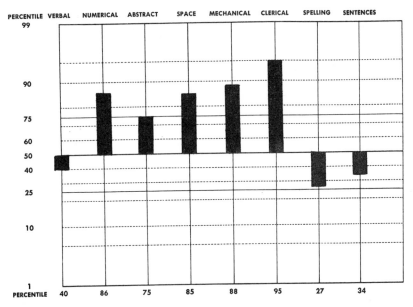

PERCENTILE	VERBAL	NUMERICAL	ABSTRACT	SPACE	MECHANICAL	CLERICAL	SPELLING	SENTENCES
PERCENTILE	40	86	75	85	88	95	27	34

not feel their job is done when they have told their counselees what the facts are and what aspirations seem reasonable. Since a boy or girl normally will agree with what has been said and will leave with a smile and a handshake, the counselor cannot assume that no more is needed to modify the directions of a person's life. Actually, we do not know whether Doris really was a timid, daydreaming girl in need of changes in her basic feelings, or whether she was mainly a misinformed girl to whom algebra sounded mysterious and very hard. Whatever the process the counselor used, it apparently was satisfactory since she now is carrying the higher-level load well.

DATE

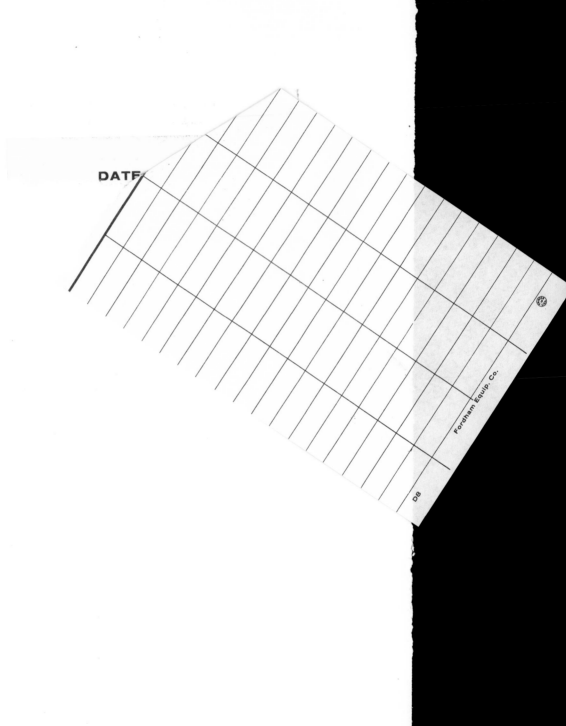

Fordham Equip. Co.

D 8